studysync®

Reading & Writing Companion

Conflicts and Clashes

When do differences become conflicts?

∷studysync®

studysync.com

ISBN 978-1-94-469579-8

4 5 6 7 8 9 LMN 24 23 22 21 20

B

Student Guide

Getting Started

Welcome to the StudySync Reading & Writing Companion! In this book, you will find a collection of readings based on the theme of the unit you are studying. As you work through the readings, you will be asked to answer questions and perform a variety of tasks designed to help you closely analyze and understand each text selection. Read on for an explanation of each section of this book.

Close Reading and Writing Routine

In each unit, you will read texts that share a common theme, despite their different genres, time periods, and authors. Each reading encourages a closer look through questions and a short writing assignment.

1 Introduction

An Introduction to each text provides historical context for your reading as well as information about the author. You will also learn about the genre of the text and the year in which it was written.

2 Notes

Many times, while working through the activities after each text, you will be asked to **annotate** or **make annotations** about what you are reading. This means that you should highlight or underline words in the text and use the "Notes" column to make comments or jot down any questions you have. You may also want to note any unfamiliar vocabulary words here.

You will also see sample student annotations to go along with the Skill lesson for that text.

3 First Read

During your first reading of each selection, you should just try to get a general idea of the content and message of the reading. Don't worry if there are parts you don't understand or words that are unfamiliar to you. You'll have an opportunity later to dive deeper into the text.

4 Think Questions

These questions will ask you to start thinking critically about the text, asking specific questions about its purpose, and making connections to your prior knowledge and reading experiences. To answer these questions, you should go back to the text and draw upon specific evidence to support your responses. You will also begin to explore some of the more challenging vocabulary words in the selection.

5 Skills

Each Skill includes two parts: Checklist and Your Turn. In the Checklist, you will learn the process for analyzing the text. The model student annotations in the text provide examples of how you might make your own notes following the instructions in the Checklist. In the Your Turn, you will use those same instructions to practice the skill.

3 RIKKI-TIKKI-TAVI First Read

studysync●

Read "Rikki-Tikki-Tavi." After you read, complete the Think Questions below.

4 THINK QUESTIONS

1. How did Rikki-tikki come to live with the English family? Cite specific evidence from the text to support your answer.

2. What do the descriptions of Nag and the dialogue in paragraphs 23–24 suggest about Nag's character? Cite specific evidence from the text to support your answer.

3. Describe in two to three sentences how Rikki-tikki saves the family from snakes.

4. Find the word **cultivated** in paragraph 18 of "Rikki-Tikki-Tavi." Use context clues in the surrounding sentences, as well as the sentence in which the word appears, to determine the word's meaning. Write your definition here and identify clues that helped you figure out the word's meaning.

5. Use context clues to determine the meaning of **sensible** as it is used in paragraph 79 of "Rikki-Tikki-Tavi." Write your definition of *sensible* here and identify clues that helped you figure out the meaning. Then check the meaning in the dictionary.

5 CHARACTER Skill: Character

Use the Checklist to analyze Character in "Rikki-Tikki-Tavi." Refer to the sample student annotations about Character in the text.

••• CHECKLIST FOR CHARACTER

In order to determine how particular elements of a story or drama interact, note the following:

- ✓ the characters in the story, including the protagonist and antagonist
- ✓ the settings and how they shape the characters or plot
- ✓ plot events and how they affect the characters
- ✓ key events or series of episodes in the plot, especially events that cause characters to react, respond, or change in some way
- ✓ characters' responses as the plot reaches a climax and moves toward a resolution of the problem facing the protagonist
- ✓ the resolution of the conflict in the plot and the ways that affects each character

To analyze how particular elements of a story or drama interact, consider the following questions:

- ✓ How do the characters' responses change or develop from the beginning to the end of the story?
- ✓ How does the setting shape the characters and plot in the story?
- ✓ How do the events in the plot affect the characters? How do they develop as a result of the conflict, climax, and resolution?
- ✓ Do the characters' problems reach a resolution? How?

↻ YOUR TURN

1. How does the mother's love for her son affect her actions in paragraph 37?

   ○ A. It prompts her to keep her son away from Rikki-tikki.
   ○ B. It causes a disagreement between her and her husband.
   ○ C. It makes her show affection towards Rikki-tikki.
   ○ D. It makes Rikki-tikki feel nervous staying with the family.

2. What does the dialogue in paragraph 40 suggest about Chuchundra?

   ○ A. He is afraid.
   ○ B. He is easily fooled.
   ○ C. He is optimistic.
   ○ D. He loves Rikki-tikki.

3. Which paragraph shows that Teddy looks to Rikki-tikki for protection?

   ○ A. 37
   ○ B. 38
   ○ C. 39
   ○ D. 40

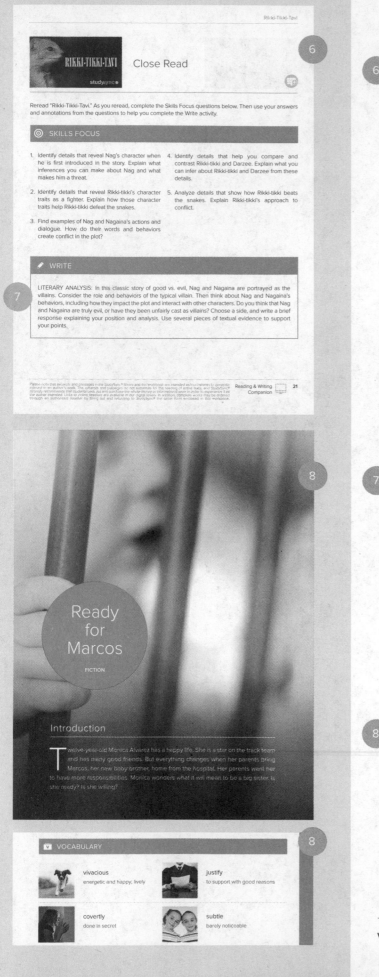

Close Read & Skills Focus

After you have completed the First Read, you will be asked to go back and read the text more closely and critically. Before you begin your Close Read, you should read through the Skills Focus to get an idea of the concepts you will want to focus on during your second reading. You should work through the Skills Focus by making annotations, highlighting important concepts, and writing notes or questions in the "Notes" column. Depending on instructions from your teacher, you may need to respond online or use a separate piece of paper to start expanding on your thoughts and ideas.

Write

Your study of each selection will end with a writing assignment. For this assignment, you should use your notes, annotations, personal ideas, and answers to both the Think and Skills Focus questions. Be sure to read the prompt carefully and address each part of it in your writing.

English Language Learner

The English Language Learner texts focus on improving language proficiency. You will practice learning strategies and skills in individual and group activities to become better readers, writers, and speakers.

Extended Writing Project and Grammar

This is your opportunity to use genre characteristics and craft to compose meaningful, longer written works exploring the theme of each unit. You will draw information from your readings, research, and own life experiences to complete the assignment.

1 Writing Project

After you have read all of the unit text selections, you will move on to a writing project. Each project will guide you through the process of writing your essay. Student models will provide guidance and help you organize your thoughts. One unit ends with an **Extended Oral Project,** which will give you an opportunity to develop your oral language and communication skills.

1 Extended Writing Project and Grammar

EXTENDED WRITING PROJECT NARRATIVE WRITING

2 Writing Process Steps

There are four steps in the writing process: Plan, Draft, Revise, and Edit and Publish. During each step, you will form and shape your writing project, and each lesson's peer review will give you the chance to receive feedback from your peers and teacher.

Extended Writing Project and Grammar

2 NARRATIVE WRITING PROCESS PLAN

Narrative Writing Process: Plan

| PLAN | DRAFT | REVISE | EDIT AND PUBLISH |

3 Writing Skills

Each Skill lesson focuses on a specific strategy or technique that you will use during your writing project. Each lesson presents a process for applying the skill to your own work and gives you the opportunity to practice it to improve your writing.

Extended Writing Project and Grammar

3 ORGANIZING NARRATIVE WRITING

Skill: Organizing Narrative Writing

••• CHECKLIST FOR ORGANIZING NARRATIVE WRITING

As you consider how to organize your narrative, use the following questions as a guide:

- Who is the narrator and who are the characters in the story?
- From what point of view will the story be told?
- Where will the story take place?
- What conflict or problem will the characters have to resolve?
- Does my plot flow logically and naturally from one event to the next?

Conflicts and Clashes

When do differences become conflicts?

> Genre Focus: FICTION

Texts

Paired Readings

Extended Writing Project and Grammar

Unit 1: Conflicts and Clashes
When do differences become conflicts?

LANGSTON HUGHES

A leader of the Harlem Renaissance, Langston Hughes (1902–1967) was born in Joplin, Missouri, and raised by his grandmother until he was sixteen. Then he moved to Lincoln, Illinois, with his mother and her husband and began to write. He eventually moved to New York City, attended Columbia University, and worked various jobs, including one on a freight ship that sailed down the coast of Africa. Hughes was first published in 1921, with "The Negro Speaks of Rivers" in the pages of *The Crisis*. He'd go on to write eleven plays and numerous works of prose and poetry.

RUDYARD KIPLING

Joseph Rudyard Kipling (1865–1936) was the first English-language writer to be awarded the Nobel Prize for Literature. Born in Bombay, India, Kipling wrote *The Jungle Book* in addition to many short stories and poems, including "Gunga Din" and "The White Man's Burden." While regarded by Henry James as a "complete man of genius," George Orwell and others have since sharply criticized Kipling's views and positions on matters of race and colonialism.

NAOMI SHIHAB NYE

A self-professed "wandering poet," Naomi Shihab Nye (b. 1952) was born to a Palestinian father and an American mother in St. Louis, Missouri; as she was growing up, she also spent time in Jerusalem and San Antonio. She has written or edited over thirty volumes of poetry, including her work *You & Yours*, a best seller. As one juror wrote before Nye won the NSK Neustadt Prize for Children's Literature, "Naomi's incandescent humanity and voice can change the world, or someone's world, by taking a position not one word less beautiful than an exquisite poem."

GARY PAULSEN

Born in Minneapolis, Minnesota, while his father served in the army overseas, Gary Paulsen (b. 1939) didn't meet his father until the age of seven. At age 16, Paulsen fled a home riven by alcoholism to work on a beet farm in North Dakota. Author of *Hatchet*, *Dogsong*, and *Winterdance*, Paulsen has written several coming-of-age stories that focus on the outdoors and the importance of nature. Paulsen has competed in the Iditarod Trail Sled Dog Race and is also an avid sailor. He has a home in Alaska.

ROD SERLING

Rod Serling (1924–1975), may be best known for hosting the television classic anthology series *The Twilight Zone*. But Serling also wrote more than half of the show's 151 episodes, in addition to writing several movies including *The Planet of the Apes*. Serling served in World War II, during which he fought in the Pacific and was awarded the Purple Heart. His wartime experience informed his activism against the Vietnam War later in life.

GARY SOTO

Growing up in California's San Joaquin Valley, Gary Soto (b. 1952) chopped beets and picked grapes in the fields outside his hometown of Fresno to help his family make ends meet. Born to Mexican American parents, Gary lost his father when he was just five years old. He worked and went to college, eventually earning his MFA from the University of California, Irvine. He has published many works of both prose and poetry, including "Oranges," the most anthologized poem in contemporary literature. He lives in Northern California.

JERRY SPINELLI

Jerry Spinelli (b. 1941) has written over thirty books but may be best known for writing *Stargirl*. The story's nonconformist theme resonated so strongly that loyal fans have created their very own "Stargirl Societies" in honor of the title character because she embraces difference as a strength. A film adaptation of the book, produced by Disney, is forthcoming. Spinelli attended Gettysburg College and began writing during his off-time while working on a department store magazine. He lives in Pennsylvania.

NOELLE STEVENSON

Noelle Stevenson (b. 1991) created the eponymous star of her groundbreaking fantasy comic *Nimona* as part of an assignment while still in college. Stevenson worked on the webcomic during her junior year at the Maryland Institute College of Art and turned it into her senior thesis. A literary agent signed her after seeing *Nimona* online, and in 2015, HarperCollins published her work as a graphic novel. Stevenson is also the creator, executive producer, and showrunner of an animated series, "She-Ra and the Princesses of Power." She lives in Los Angeles.

OSCAR CASARES

Brownsville is both the hometown of Oscar Casares (b. 1964) and the title of his debut collection. Brownsville was published by Little, Brown in 2003, just after Casares finished his MFA at the University of Iowa Writers' Workshop. Asked how he became a writer, Casares once said, "I grew up around uncles who were storytellers and so I kind of continued the tradition with family and friends. Then one day I tried to write some of these stories and ended up with completely new ones." He teaches at the University of Texas, his alma mater.

SHARON G. FLAKE

Sharon G. Flake (b. 1955) wrote her bestselling debut novel, *The Skin I'm In*, while working in public relations for a university press. Born in Philadelphia, she earned her Bachelor of Arts degree in English at the University of Plttsburgh where she also minored in Political Science and wrote for the *Pitt News*. After graduation, she took a job at an area youth shelter. During that time, she began work on her bestseller, which also won many awards, including the Coretta Scott King/John Steptoe Award for New Talent. She lives in Pittsburgh.

YOSHIKO UCHIDA

During her senior year at University of California, Berkeley, Yoshiko Uchida (1921–1992) and her family were imprisoned in internment camps for three years in the American West. These events inspired her volume of memoirs, *Desert Exile: The Uprooting of a Japanese American Family*, published in 1982. Her nephew, writer Michiko Kakutani, said that she wrote "with the hope that through knowledge of the past, [our nation] will never allow another group of people in America to be sent into a desert exile ever again." Uchida authored twenty-seven books. She was born in Alameda, California.

Rikki-Tikki-Tavi

FICTION
Rudyard Kipling
1894

Introduction

"Rikki-Tikki-Tavi" is one of the most famous tales from *The Jungle Book*, a collection of short stories published in 1894 by English author Rudyard Kipling (1865–1936). The stories in *The Jungle Book* feature animal characters with anthropomorphic traits and are intended to be read as fables, each illustrating a moral lesson. In this story, Rikki-tikki-tavi is a courageous young mongoose adopted as a pet by a British family living in 19th-century colonial India.

"Rikki-tikki held on with his eyes shut, for now he was quite sure he was dead."

1   This is the story of the great war that Rikki-tikki-tavi fought single-handed, through the bath-rooms of the big bungalow in Segowlee cantonment. Darzee, the Tailorbird, helped him, and Chuchundra, the musk-rat, who never comes out into the middle of the floor, but always creeps round by the wall, gave him advice, but Rikki-tikki did the real fighting.

2   He was a mongoose, rather like a little cat in his fur and his tail, but quite like a weasel in his head and his habits. His eyes and the end of his restless nose were pink. He could scratch himself anywhere he pleased with any leg, front or back, that he chose to use. He could fluff up his tail till it looked like a bottle brush, and his war cry as he scuttled through the long grass was: "Rikk-tikk-tikki-tikki-tchk!"

3   One day, a high summer flood washed him out of the burrow where he lived with his father and mother, and carried him, kicking and clucking, down a roadside ditch. He found a little wisp of grass floating there, and clung to it till he lost his senses. When he revived, he was lying in the hot sun on the middle of a garden path, very draggled indeed, and a small boy was saying, "Here's a dead mongoose. Let's have a funeral."

4   "No," said his mother, "let's take him in and dry him. Perhaps he isn't really dead."

5   They took him into the house, and a big man picked him up between his finger and thumb and said he was not dead but half choked. So they wrapped him in cotton wool, and warmed him over a little fire, and he opened his eyes and sneezed.

6   "Now," said the big man (he was an Englishman who had just moved into the bungalow), "don't frighten him, and we'll see what he'll do."

7   It is the hardest thing in the world to frighten a mongoose, because he is eaten up from nose to tail with curiosity. The motto of all the mongoose family is "Run and find out," and Rikki-tikki was a true mongoose. He looked at the cotton wool, decided that it was not good to eat, ran all round the table, sat up and put his fur in order, scratched himself, and jumped on the small boy's shoulder.

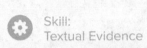

Skill:
Textual Evidence

It says that he fluffs up his tail and he has a war cry. I know that a war cry is used in battle to rally the troops. This must mean that Rikki-tikki is brave and powerful, like a soldier.

Skill:
Text-Dependent Responses

After finding Rikki-tikki, the English family brought him into their home and took care of him.

Reading & Writing
Companion

NOTES

8   "Don't be frightened, Teddy," said his father. "That's his way of making friends."

9   "Ouch! He's tickling under my chin," said Teddy.

10 Rikki-tikki looked down between the boy's collar and neck, snuffed at his ear, and climbed down to the floor, where he sat rubbing his nose.

11 "Good gracious," said Teddy's mother, "and that's a wild creature! I suppose he's so tame because we've been kind to him."

12 "All mongooses are like that," said her husband. "If Teddy doesn't pick him up by the tail, or try to put him in a cage, he'll run in and out of the house all day long. Let's give him something to eat."

13 They gave him a little piece of raw meat. Rikki-tikki liked it **immensely**, and when it was finished he went out into the veranda and sat in the sunshine and fluffed up his fur to make it dry to the roots. Then he felt better.

14 "There are more things to find out about in this house," he said to himself, "than all my family could find out in all their lives. I shall certainly stay and find out."

15 He spent all that day roaming over the house. He nearly drowned himself in the bath-tubs, put his nose into the ink on a writing table, and burned it on the end of the big man's cigar, for he climbed up in the big man's lap to see how writing was done. At nightfall he ran into Teddy's nursery to watch how kerosene lamps were lighted, and when Teddy went to bed Rikki-tikki climbed up too. But he was a restless companion, because he had to get up and attend to every noise all through the night, and find out what made it. Teddy's mother and father came in, the last thing, to look at their boy, and Rikki-tikki was awake on the pillow. "I don't like that," said Teddy's mother. "He may bite the child." "He'll do no such thing," said the father. "Teddy's safer with that little beast than if he had a bloodhound to watch him. If a snake came into the nursery now—"

16 But Teddy's mother wouldn't think of anything so awful.

17 Early in the morning Rikki-tikki came to early breakfast in the veranda riding on Teddy's shoulder, and they gave him banana and some boiled egg. He sat on all their laps one after the other, because every well-brought-up mongoose always hopes to be a house mongoose some day and have rooms to run about in; and Rikki-tikki's mother (she used to live in the general's house at Segowlee) had carefully told Rikki what to do if ever he came across white men.

18 Then Rikki-tikki went out into the garden to see what was to be seen. It was a large garden, only half **cultivated**, with bushes, as big as summer-houses, of Marshal Niel roses, lime and orange trees, clumps of bamboos, and thickets of high grass. Rikki-tikki licked his lips. "This is a splendid hunting-ground," he said, and his tail grew bottle-brushy at the thought of it, and he scuttled up

NOTES

and down the garden, snuffing here and there till he heard very sorrowful voices in a thorn-bush.

19 It was Darzee, the Tailorbird, and his wife. They had made a beautiful nest by pulling two big leaves together and stitching them up the edges with fibers, and had filled the hollow with cotton and downy fluff. The nest swayed to and fro, as they sat on the rim and cried.

20 "What is the matter?" asked Rikki-tikki.

21 "We are very miserable," said Darzee. "One of our babies fell out of the nest yesterday and Nag ate him."

22 "H'm!" said Rikki-tikki, "that is very sad—but I am a stranger here. Who is Nag?"

23 Darzee and his wife only cowered down in the nest without answering, for from the thick grass at the foot of the bush there came a low hiss—a horrid cold sound that made Rikki-tikki jump back two clear feet. Then inch by inch out of the grass rose up the head and spread hood of Nag, the big black cobra, and he was five feet long from tongue to tail. When he had lifted one-third of himself clear of the ground, he stayed balancing to and fro exactly as a dandelion tuft balances in the wind, and he looked at Rikki-tikki with the wicked snake's eyes that never change their expression, whatever the snake may be thinking of.

24 "Who is Nag?" said he. "I am Nag. The great God Brahm[1] put his mark upon all our people, when the first cobra spread his hood to keep the sun off Brahm as he slept. Look, and be afraid!"

25 He spread out his hood more than ever, and Rikki-tikki saw the spectacle-mark on the back of it that looks exactly like the eye part of a hook-and-eye fastening. He was afraid for the minute, but it is impossible for a mongoose to stay frightened for any length of time, and though Rikki-tikki had never met a live cobra before, his mother had fed him on dead ones, and he knew that all a grown mongoose's business in life was to fight and eat snakes. Nag knew that too and, at the bottom of his cold heart, he was afraid.

26 "Well," said Rikki-tikki, and his tail began to fluff up again, "marks or no marks, do you think it is right for you to eat fledglings out of a nest?"

27 Nag was thinking to himself, and watching the least little movement in the grass behind Rikki-tikki. He knew that mongooses in the garden meant death sooner or later for him and his family, but he wanted to get Rikki-tikki off his guard. So he dropped his head a little, and put it on one side.

28 "Let us talk," he said. "You eat eggs. Why should not I eat birds?"

Skill:
Character

Rikki-tikki is ready to fight a cobra to protect the birds he just met. He's loyal and protective. I think Rikki-tikki's loyalty will lead to danger or success in the plot.

---

1. **Brahm** in Hindu tradition, one of the gods of creation. (Another spelling for this is *Brahma*.)

29   "Behind you! Look behind you!" sang Darzee.

30   Rikki-tikki knew better than to waste time in staring. He jumped up in the air as high as he could go, and just under him whizzed by the head of Nagaina, Nag's wicked wife. She had crept up behind him as he was talking, to make an end of him. He heard her savage hiss as the stroke missed. He came down almost across her back, and if he had been an old mongoose he would have known that then was the time to break her back with one bite; but he was afraid of the terrible lashing return stroke of the cobra. He bit, indeed, but did not bite long enough, and he jumped clear of the whisking tail, leaving Nagaina torn and angry.

31   "Wicked, wicked Darzee!" said Nag, lashing up as high as he could reach toward the nest in the thorn-bush. But Darzee had built it out of reach of snakes, and it only swayed to and fro.

32   Rikki-tikki felt his eyes growing red and hot (when a mongoose's eyes grow red, he is angry), and he sat back on his tail and hind legs like a little kangaroo, and looked all round him, and chattered with rage. But Nag and Nagaina had disappeared into the grass. When a snake misses its stroke, it never says anything or gives any sign of what it means to do next. Rikki-tikki did not care to follow them, for he did not feel sure that he could manage two snakes at once. So he trotted off to the gravel path near the house, and sat down to think. It was a serious matter for him.

33   If you read the old books of natural history, you will find they say that when the mongoose fights the snake and happens to get bitten, he runs off and eats some herb that cures him. That is not true. The victory is only a matter of quickness of eye and quickness of foot—snake's blow against mongoose's jump—and as no eye can follow the motion of a snake's head when it strikes, this makes things much more wonderful than any magic herb. Rikki-tikki knew he was a young mongoose, and it made him all the more pleased to think that he had managed to escape a blow from behind. It gave him confidence in himself, and when Teddy came running down the path, Rikki-tikki was ready to be petted.

34   But just as Teddy was stooping, something wriggled a little in the dust, and a tiny voice said: "Be careful. I am Death!" It was Karait, the dusty brown snakeling that lies for choice on the dusty earth; and his bite is as dangerous as the cobra's. But he is so small that nobody thinks of him, and so he does the more harm to people.

35 Rikki-tikki's eyes grew red again, and he danced up to Karait with the peculiar rocking, swaying motion that he had inherited from his family. It looks very funny, but it is so perfectly balanced a gait that you can fly off from it at any angle you please, and in dealing with snakes this is an advantage. If Rikki-tikki had only known, he was doing a much more dangerous thing than fighting Nag, for Karait is so small, and can turn so quickly, that unless Rikki bit him close to the back of the head, he would get the return stroke in his eye or his lip. But Rikki did not know. His eyes were all red, and he rocked back and forth, looking for a good place to hold. Karait struck out. Rikki jumped sideways and tried to run in, but the wicked little dusty gray head lashed within a fraction of his shoulder, and he had to jump over the body, and the head followed his heels close.

36 Teddy shouted to the house: "Oh, look here! Our mongoose is killing a snake." And Rikki-tikki heard a scream from Teddy's mother. His father ran out with a stick, but by the time he came up, Karait had lunged out once too far, and Rikki-tikki had sprung, jumped on the snake's back, dropped his head far between his forelegs, bitten as high up the back as he could get hold, and rolled away. That bite paralyzed Karait, and Rikki-tikki was just going to eat him up from the tail, after the custom of his family at dinner, when he remembered that a full meal makes a slow mongoose, and if he wanted all his strength and quickness ready, he must keep himself thin.

37 He went away for a dust bath under the castor-oil bushes, while Teddy's father beat the dead Karait. "What is the use of that?" thought Rikki-tikki. "I have settled it all;" and then Teddy's mother picked him up from the dust and hugged him, crying that he had saved Teddy from death, and Teddy's father said that he was a **providence**, and Teddy looked on with big scared eyes. Rikki-tikki was rather amused at all the fuss, which, of course, he did not understand. Teddy's mother might just as well have petted Teddy for playing in the dust. Rikki was thoroughly enjoying himself.

38 That night at dinner, walking to and fro among the wine-glasses on the table, he might have stuffed himself three times over with nice things. But he remembered Nag and Nagaina, and though it was very pleasant to be patted and petted by Teddy's mother, and to sit on Teddy's shoulder, his eyes would get red from time to time, and he would go off into his long war cry of "Rikk-tikk-tikki-tikki-tchk!"

39 Teddy carried him off to bed, and insisted on Rikki-tikki sleeping under his chin. Rikki-tikki was too well bred to bite or scratch, but as soon as Teddy was asleep he went off for his nightly walk round the house, and in the dark he ran up against Chuchundra, the musk-rat, creeping around by the wall. Chuchundra is a broken-hearted little beast. He whimpers and cheeps all the night, trying to make up his mind to run into the middle of the room. But he never gets there.

40   "Don't kill me," said Chuchundra, almost weeping. "Rikki-tikki, don't kill me!"

41   "Do you think a snake-killer kills muskrats?" said Rikki-tikki scornfully.

42   "Those who kill snakes get killed by snakes," said Chuchundra, more sorrowfully than ever. "And how am I to be sure that Nag won't mistake me for you some dark night?"

43   "There's not the least danger," said Rikki-tikki. "But Nag is in the garden, and I know you don't go there."

44   "My cousin Chua, the rat, told me—" said Chuchundra, and then he stopped.

45   "Told you what?"

46   "H'sh! Nag is everywhere, Rikki-tikki. You should have talked to Chua in the garden."

47   "I didn't—so you must tell me. Quick, Chuchundra, or I'll bite you!"

48   Chuchundra sat down and cried till the tears rolled off his whiskers. "I am a very poor man," he sobbed. "I never had spirit enough to run out into the middle of the room. H'sh! I mustn't tell you anything. Can't you hear, Rikki-tikki?"

49   Rikki-tikki listened. The house was as still as still, but he thought he could just catch the faintest scratch-scratch in the world—a noise as faint as that of a wasp walking on a window-pane—the dry scratch of a snake's scales on brick-work.

50   "That's Nag or Nagaina," he said to himself, "and he is crawling into the bath-room sluice[2]. You're right, Chuchundra; I should have talked to Chua."

51   He stole off to Teddy's bath-room, but there was nothing there, and then to Teddy's mother's bathroom. At the bottom of the smooth plaster wall there was a brick pulled out to make a sluice for the bath water, and as Rikki-tikki stole in by the masonry curb where the bath is put, he heard Nag and Nagaina whispering together outside in the moonlight.

52   "When the house is emptied of people," said Nagaina to her husband, "he will have to go away, and then the garden will be our own again. Go in quietly, and remember that the big man who killed Karait is the first one to bite. Then come out and tell me, and we will hunt for Rikki-tikki together."

53   "But are you sure that there is anything to be gained by killing the people?" said Nag.

54   "Everything. When there were no people in the bungalow, did we have any mongoose in the garden? So long as the bungalow is empty, we are king and

---

2. **sluice** a channel for the flow of water, regulated at its head by a gate

queen of the garden; and remember that as soon as our eggs in the melon bed hatch (as they may tomorrow), our children will need room and quiet."

55 "I had not thought of that," said Nag. "I will go, but there is no need that we should hunt for Rikki-tikki afterward. I will kill the big man and his wife, and the child if I can, and come away quietly. Then the bungalow will be empty, and Rikki-tikki will go."

56 Rikki-tikki tingled all over with rage and hatred at this, and then Nag's head came through the sluice, and his five feet of cold body followed it. Angry as he was, Rikki-tikki was very frightened as he saw the size of the big cobra. Nag coiled himself up, raised his head, and looked into the bathroom in the dark, and Rikki could see his eyes glitter.

57 "Now, if I kill him here, Nagaina will know; and if I fight him on the open floor, the odds are in his favor. What am I to do?" said Rikki-tikki-tavi.

58 Nag waved to and fro, and then Rikki-tikki heard him drinking from the biggest water-jar that was used to fill the bath. "That is good," said the snake. "Now, when Karait was killed, the big man had a stick. He may have that stick still, but when he comes in to bathe in the morning he will not have a stick. I shall wait here till he comes. Nagaina—do you hear me?—I shall wait here in the cool till daytime."

59 There was no answer from outside, so Rikki-tikki knew Nagaina had gone away. Nag coiled himself down, coil by coil, round the bulge at the bottom of the water-jar, and Rikki-tikki stayed still as death. After an hour he began to move, muscle by muscle, toward the jar. Nag was asleep, and Rikki-tikki looked at his big back, wondering which would be the best place for a good hold. "If I don't break his back at the first jump," said Rikki, "he can still fight. And if he fights—O Rikki!" He looked at the thickness of the neck below the hood, but that was too much for him; and a bite near the tail would only make Nag savage.

60 "It must be the head," he said at last; "the head above the hood. And, when I am once there, I must not let go."

61 Then he jumped. The head was lying a little clear of the water jar, under the curve of it; and, as his teeth met, Rikki braced his back against the bulge of the red earthenware to hold down the head. This gave him just one second's purchase, and he made the most of it. Then he was battered to and fro as a rat is shaken by a dog—to and fro on the floor, up and down, and around in great circles, but his eyes were red and he held on as the body cart-whipped over the floor, upsetting the tin dipper and the soap dish and the flesh brush, and banged against the tin side of the bath. As he held he closed his jaws tighter and tighter, for he made sure he would be banged to death, and, for the honor of his family, he preferred to be found with his teeth locked. He was

Please note that excerpts and passages in the StudySync® library and this workbook are intended as touchstones to generate interest in an author's work. The excerpts and passages do not substitute for the reading of entire texts, and StudySync® strongly recommends that students seek out and purchase the whole literary or informational work in order to experience it as the author intended. Links to online resellers are available in our digital library. In addition, complete works may be ordered through an authorized reseller by filling out and returning to StudySync® the order form enclosed in this workbook.

Reading & Writing Companion

7

dizzy, aching, and felt shaken to pieces when something went off like a thunderclap just behind him. A hot wind knocked him senseless and red fire singed his fur. The big man had been wakened by the noise, and had fired both barrels of a shotgun into Nag just behind the hood.

62 Rikki-tikki held on with his eyes shut, for now he was quite sure he was dead. But the head did not move, and the big man picked him up and said, "It's the mongoose again, Alice. The little chap has saved our lives now."

63 Then Teddy's mother came in with a very white face, and saw what was left of Nag, and Rikki-tikki dragged himself to Teddy's bedroom and spent half the rest of the night shaking himself tenderly to find out whether he really was broken into forty pieces, as he fancied.

64 When morning came he was very stiff, but well pleased with his doings. "Now I have Nagaina to settle with, and she will be worse than five Nags, and there's no knowing when the eggs she spoke of will hatch. Goodness! I must go and see Darzee," he said.

65 Without waiting for breakfast, Rikki-tikki ran to the thornbush where Darzee was singing a song of triumph at the top of his voice. The news of Nag's death was all over the garden, for the sweeper had thrown the body on the rubbish[3]-heap.

66 "Oh, you stupid tuft of feathers!" said Rikki-tikki angrily. "Is this the time to sing?"

67 "Nag is dead—is dead—is dead!" sang Darzee. "The valiant Rikki-tikki caught him by the head and held fast. The big man brought the bang-stick, and Nag fell in two pieces! He will never eat my babies again."

68 "All that's true enough. But where's Nagaina?" said Rikki-tikki, looking carefully round him.

69 "Nagaina came to the bathroom sluice and called for Nag," Darzee went on, "and Nag came out on the end of a stick—the sweeper picked him up on the end of a stick and threw him upon the rubbish heap. Let us sing about the great, the red-eyed Rikki-tikki!" And Darzee filled his throat and sang.

70 "If I could get up to your nest, I'd roll your babies out!" said Rikki-tikki. "You don't know when to do the right thing at the right time. You're safe enough in your nest there, but it's war for me down here. Stop singing a minute, Darzee."

71 "For the great, the beautiful Rikki-tikki's sake I will stop," said Darzee. "What is it, O Killer of the terrible Nag?"

_____

3. **rubbish** waste or trash

72 "Where is Nagaina, for the third time?"

73 "On the rubbish heap by the stables, mourning for Nag. Great is Rikki-tikki with the white teeth."

74 "Bother my white teeth! Have you ever heard where she keeps her eggs?"

75 "In the melon bed, on the end nearest the wall, where the sun strikes nearly all day. She hid them there weeks ago."

76 "And you never thought it worth while to tell me? The end nearest the wall, you said?"

77 "Rikki-tikki, you are not going to eat her eggs?"

78 "Not eat exactly; no. Darzee, if you have a grain of sense you will fly off to the stables and pretend that your wing is broken, and let Nagaina chase you away to this bush. I must get to the melon-bed, and if I went there now she'd see me."

79 Darzee was a feather-brained little fellow who could never hold more than one idea at a time in his head. And just because he knew that Nagaina's children were born in eggs like his own, he didn't think at first that it was fair to kill them. But his wife was a **sensible** bird, and she knew that cobra's eggs meant young cobras later on. So she flew off from the nest, and left Darzee to keep the babies warm, and continue his song about the death of Nag. Darzee was very like a man in some ways.

80 She fluttered in front of Nagaina by the rubbish heap and cried out, "Oh, my wing is broken! The boy in the house threw a stone at me and broke it." Then she fluttered more desperately than ever.

81 Nagaina lifted up her head and hissed, "You warned Rikki-tikki when I would have killed him. Indeed and truly, you've chosen a bad place to be lame in." And she moved toward Darzee's wife, slipping along over the dust.

82 "The boy broke it with a stone!" shrieked Darzee's wife.

83 "Well! It may be some **consolation** to you when you're dead to know that I shall settle accounts with the boy. My husband lies on the rubbish heap this morning, but before night the boy in the house will lie very still. What is the use of running away? I am sure to catch you. Little fool, look at me!"

84 Darzee's wife knew better than to do that, for a bird who looks at a snake's eyes gets so frightened that she cannot move. Darzee's wife fluttered on, piping sorrowfully, and never leaving the ground, and Nagaina quickened her pace.

85 Rikki-tikki heard them going up the path from the stables, and he raced for the end of the melon patch near the wall. There, in the warm litter above the

NOTES

melons, very cunningly hidden, he found twenty-five eggs, about the size of a bantam's eggs, but with whitish skin instead of shell.

86   "I was not a day too soon," he said, for he could see the baby cobras curled up inside the skin, and he knew that the minute they were hatched they could each kill a man or a mongoose. He bit off the tops of the eggs as fast as he could, taking care to crush the young cobras, and turned over the litter from time to time to see whether he had missed any. At last there were only three eggs left, and Rikki-tikki began to chuckle to himself, when he heard Darzee's wife screaming:

87   "Rikki-tikki, I led Nagaina toward the house, and she has gone into the veranda, and—oh, come quickly—she means killing!"

88   Rikki-tikki smashed two eggs, and tumbled backward down the melon-bed with the third egg in his mouth, and scuttled to the veranda as hard as he could put foot to the ground. Teddy and his mother and father were there at early breakfast, but Rikki-tikki saw that they were not eating anything. They sat stone-still, and their faces were white. Nagaina was coiled up on the matting by Teddy's chair, within easy striking distance of Teddy's bare leg, and she was swaying to and fro, singing a song of triumph.

89   "Son of the big man that killed Nag," she hissed, "stay still. I am not ready yet. Wait a little. Keep very still, all you three! If you move I strike, and if you do not move I strike. Oh, foolish people, who killed my Nag!"

90   Teddy's eyes were fixed on his father, and all his father could do was to whisper, "Sit still, Teddy. You mustn't move. Teddy, keep still."

91   Then Rikki-tikki came up and cried, "Turn round, Nagaina. Turn and fight!"

92   "All in good time," said she, without moving her eyes. "I will settle my account with you presently. Look at your friends, Rikki-tikki. They are still and white. They are afraid. They dare not move, and if you come a step nearer I strike."

93   "Look at your eggs," said Rikki-tikki, "in the melon bed near the wall. Go and look, Nagaina!"

94   The big snake turned half around, and saw the egg on the veranda. "Ah-h! Give it to me," she said.

95   Rikki-tikki put his paws one on each side of the egg, and his eyes were blood-red. "What price for a snake's egg? For a young cobra? For a young king cobra? For the last—the very last of the brood? The ants are eating all the others down by the melon bed."

96   Nagaina spun clear round, forgetting everything for the sake of the one egg. Rikki-tikki saw Teddy's father shoot out a big hand, catch Teddy by the

shoulder, and drag him across the little table with the tea-cups, safe and out of reach of Nagaina.

97 "Tricked! Tricked! Tricked! Rikk-tck-tck!" chuckled Rikki-tikki. "The boy is safe, and it was I—I—I that caught Nag by the hood last night in the bathroom," Then he began to jump up and down, all four feet together, his head close to the floor. "He threw me to and fro, but he could not shake me off. He was dead before the big man blew him in two. I did it! Rikki-tikki-tck-tck! Come then, Nagaina. Come and fight with me. You shall not be a widow long."

98 Nagaina saw that she had lost her chance of killing Teddy, and the egg lay between Rikki-tikki's paws. "Give me the egg, Rikki-tikki. Give me the last of my eggs, and I will go away and never come back," she said, lowering her hood.

99 "Yes, you will go away, and you will never come back. For you will go to the rubbish heap with Nag. Fight, widow! The big man has gone for his gun! Fight!"

100 Rikki-tikki was bounding all round Nagaina, keeping just out of reach of her stroke, his little eyes like hot coals. Nagaina gathered herself together and flung out at him. Rikki-tikki jumped up and backward. Again and again and again she struck, and each time her head came with a whack on the matting of the veranda and she gathered herself together like a watch spring. Then Rikki-tikki danced in a circle to get behind her, and Nagaina spun round to keep her head to his head, so that the rustle of her tail on the matting sounded like dry leaves blown along by the wind.

101 He had forgotten the egg. It still lay on the veranda, and Nagaina came nearer and nearer to it, till at last, while Rikki-tikki was drawing breath, she caught it in her mouth, turned to the veranda steps, and flew like an arrow down the path, with Rikki-tikki behind her. When the cobra runs for her life, she goes like a whip-lash flicked across a horse's neck.

102 Rikki-tikki knew that he must catch her, or all the trouble would begin again. She headed straight for the long grass by the thorn-bush, and as he was running Rikki-tikki heard Darzee still singing his foolish little song of triumph. But Darzee's wife was wiser. She flew off her nest as Nagaina came along, and flapped her wings about Nagaina's head. If Darzee had helped they might have turned her, but Nagaina only lowered her hood and went on. Still, the instant's delay brought Rikki-tikki up to her, and as she plunged into the rat-hole where she and Nag used to live, his little white teeth were clenched on her tail, and he went down with her—and very few mongooses, however wise and old they may be, care to follow a cobra into its hole. It was dark in the hole; and Rikki-tikki never knew when it might open out and give Nagaina room to turn and strike at him. He held on savagely, and stuck out his feet to act as brakes on the dark slope of the hot, moist earth.

NOTES

103   Then the grass by the mouth of the hole stopped waving, and Darzee said, "It is all over with Rikki-tikki! We must sing his death song. Valiant Rikki-tikki is dead! For Nagaina will surely kill him underground."

104   So he sang a very mournful song that he made up on the spur of the minute, and just as he got to the most touching part, the grass quivered again, and Rikki-tikki, covered with dirt, dragged himself out of the hole leg by leg, licking his whiskers. Darzee stopped with a little shout. Rikki-tikki shook some of the dust out of his fur and sneezed. "It is all over," he said. "The widow will never come out again." And the red ants that live between the grass stems heard him, and began to troop down one after another to see if he had spoken the truth. Rikki-tikki curled himself up in the grass and slept where he was—slept and slept till it was late in the afternoon, for he had done a hard day's work.

105   "Now," he said, when he awoke, "I will go back to the house. Tell the Coppersmith, Darzee, and he will tell the garden that Nagaina is dead."

106   The Coppersmith is a bird who makes a noise exactly like the beating of a little hammer on a copper pot; and the reason he is always making it is because he is the town crier to every Indian garden, and tells all the news to everybody who cares to listen. As Rikki-tikki went up the path, he heard his "attention" notes like a tiny dinner gong, and then the steady "Ding-dong-tock! Nag is dead—dong! Nagaina is dead! Ding-dong-tock!" That set all the birds in the garden singing, and the frogs croaking, for Nag and Nagaina used to eat frogs as well as little birds.

107   When Rikki got to the house, Teddy and Teddy's mother (she looked very white still, for she had been fainting) and Teddy's father came out and almost cried over him; and that night he ate all that was given him till he could eat no more, and went to bed on Teddy's shoulder, where Teddy's mother saw him when she came to look late at night.

108   "He saved our lives and Teddy's life," she said to her husband. "Just think, he saved all our lives."

109   Rikki-tikki woke up with a jump, for the mongooses are light sleepers.

110   "Oh, it's you," said he. "What are you bothering for? All the cobras are dead. And if they weren't, I'm here."

111   Rikki-tikki had a right to be proud of himself. But he did not grow too proud, and he kept that garden as a mongoose should keep it, with tooth and jump and spring and bite, till never a cobra dared show its head inside the walls.

Reading & Writing Companion

Skill:
Text-Dependent Responses

Use the Checklist to analyze Text-Dependent Responses in "Rikki-Tikki-Tavi." Refer to the sample student annotations about Text-Dependent Responses in the text.

••• CHECKLIST FOR TEXT-DEPENDENT RESPONSES

In order to cite several pieces of textual evidence to support an analysis, consider the following:

✓ details from the text to make an inference or draw a conclusion. Inferences are logical guesses about information in a text that is not directly, or explicitly, stated by the author.

- Read carefully and consider why an author gives particular details and information.
- Think about what you already know, and use your own knowledge and experiences to help you figure out what the author does not state directly.
- Cite textual evidence, or the specific words, phrases, sentences, or paragraphs that led you to make an inference.

✓ details that you can use to support your ideas and opinions about a text

✓ explicit evidence of a character's feelings or motivations, or the reasons behind a historical event in a nonfiction text

- Explicit evidence is stated directly in the text and must be cited accurately to support a text-dependent answer or analysis.

To cite several pieces of textual evidence to support an analysis, consider the following questions:

✓ What types of textual evidence can I use to support an analysis of a text?

✓ What explicit evidence can I use to support my analysis?

✓ If I infer things in the text that the author does not state directly, what evidence from the text, along with my own experiences and knowledge, can I use to support my analysis?

✓ Have I used several pieces of textual evidence to support my analysis?

Skill:
Text-Dependent Responses

Read the second Think question from the First Read lesson for "Rikki-Tikki-Tavi" and the writer's responses below. Then, complete the chart by deciding which evidence from the text best supports each response.

↻ YOUR TURN

	Textual Evidence Options
A	Then inch by inch out of the grass rose up the head and spread hood of Nag, the big black cobra, and he was five feet long from tongue to tail.
B	Darzee and his wife only cowered down in the nest without answering, for from the thick grass at the foot of the bush there came a low hiss—a horrid cold sound that made Rikki-tikki jump back two clear feet.
C	"I am Nag. The great God Brahm put his mark upon all our people, when the first cobra spread his hood to keep the sun off Brahm as he slept. Look, and be afraid!"

Response	Textual Evidence
The other animals in the garden are afraid of Nag.	
Nag uses his size to intimidate.	
Nag's own words show how scary he is.	

First Read

RIKKI-TIKKI-TAVI

studysync ⓥ

Read "Rikki-Tikki-Tavi." After you read, complete the Think Questions below.

☁ THINK QUESTIONS

1. How did Rikki-tikki come to live with the English family? Cite specific evidence from the text to support your answer.

2. What do the descriptions of Nag and the dialogue in paragraphs 23–24 suggest about Nag's character? Cite specific evidence from the text to support your answer.

3. Describe in two to three sentences how Rikki-tikki saves the family from snakes.

4. Find the word **cultivated** in paragraph 18 of "Rikki-Tikki-Tavi." Use context clues in the surrounding sentences, as well as the sentence in which the word appears, to determine the word's meaning. Write your definition here and identify clues that helped you figure out the word's meaning.

5. Use context clues to determine the meaning of **sensible** as it is used in paragraph 79 of "Rikki-Tikki-Tavi." Write your definition of *sensible* here and identify clues that helped you figure out the meaning. Then check the meaning in the dictionary.

Please note that excerpts and passages in the StudySync® library and this workbook are intended as touchstones to generate interest in an author's work. The excerpts and passages do not substitute for the reading of entire texts, and StudySync® strongly recommends that students seek out and purchase the whole literary or informational work in order to experience it as the author intended. Links to online resellers are available in our digital library. In addition, complete works may be ordered through an authorized reseller by filling out and returning to StudySync® the order form enclosed in this workbook.

Reading & Writing Companion   15

Skill:
Textual Evidence

Use the Checklist to analyze Textual Evidence in "Rikki-Tikki-Tavi." Refer to the sample student annotations about Textual Evidence in the text.

••• CHECKLIST FOR TEXTUAL EVIDENCE

In order to support an analysis by citing textual evidence that is explicitly stated in the text, do the following:

- ✓ Read the text closely and critically.

- ✓ Identify what the text says explicitly.

- ✓ Find the most relevant textual evidence that supports your analysis.

- ✓ Consider why an author explicitly states specific details and information.

- ✓ Cite the specific words, phrases, sentences, paragraphs, or images from the text that support your analysis.

In order to interpret implicit meanings in a text by making inferences, do the following:

- ✓ Combine information directly stated in the text with your own knowledge, experiences, and observations.

- ✓ Cite the specific words, phrases, sentences, paragraphs, or images from the text that support this inference.

In order to cite textual evidence to support an analysis of what the text says explicitly as well as inferences drawn from the text, consider the following questions:

- ✓ Have I read the text closely and critically?

- ✓ What inferences am I making about the text? What textual evidence am I using to support these inferences?

- ✓ Am I quoting the evidence from the text correctly?

- ✓ Does my textual evidence logically relate to my analysis?

- ✓ Have I cited several pieces of textual evidence?

Skill:
Textual Evidence

sync•skills

Complete the chart on the following page by matching the correct background knowledge and implicit meaning with each explicit meaning.

⟳ YOUR TURN

	Background Knowledge and Implicit Meaning Options
A	I know that snakes stand up straight when they are feeling threatened. They do this to scare other animals or people.
B	Rikki-tikki scuttling reminds me of little kids going outside to play. They get so excited when they see a new park or playground. They run up and down and around.
C	Teddy and his mother and father must be scared and nervous. That's why they aren't eating.
D	Here, the author is suggesting that Rikki-tikki is brave and powerful like a hero.
E	Your face turns white when you are scared or nervous.
F	I can infer that Rikki-tikki is very excited about the idea of hunting in the garden.
G	This reminds me of a battle of heroes vs. villains from a movie or comic book.
H	It seems like the cobra might feel threatened or frightened by Rikki-tikki. He's probably sitting up tall in order to protect himself and scare away the mongoose.

Explicit Evidence	Background Knowledge	Implicit Meaning
Rikki-tikki licked his lips. "This is a splendid hunting-ground," he said, and his tail grew bottle-brushy at the thought of it, and he scuttled up and down the garden, snuffing here and there till he heard very sorrowful voices in a thorn-bush.		
When he had lifted one-third of himself clear of the ground, he stayed balancing to and fro exactly as a dandelion tuft balances in the wind, and he looked at Rikki-tikki with the wicked snake's eyes that never change their expression, whatever the snake may be thinking of.		
Rikki-tikki's eyes grew red again, and he danced up to Karait with the peculiar rocking, swaying motion that he had inherited from his family.		
Teddy and his mother and father were there at early breakfast, but Rikki-tikki saw that they were not eating anything. They sat stone-still, and their faces were white.		

Skill:
Character

Use the Checklist to analyze Character in "Rikki-Tikki-Tavi." Refer to the sample student annotations about Character in the text.

••• CHECKLIST FOR CHARACTER

In order to determine how particular elements of a story or drama interact, note the following:

- ✓ the characters in the story, including the protagonist and antagonist

- ✓ the settings and how they shape the characters or plot

- ✓ plot events and how they affect the characters

- ✓ key events or series of episodes in the plot, especially events that cause characters to react, respond, or change in some way

- ✓ characters' responses as the plot reaches a climax and moves toward a resolution of the problem facing the protagonist

- ✓ the resolution of the conflict in the plot and the ways that affects each character

To analyze how particular elements of a story or drama interact, consider the following questions:

- ✓ How do the characters' responses change or develop from the beginning to the end of the story?

- ✓ How does the setting shape the characters and plot in the story?

- ✓ How do the events in the plot affect the characters? How do they develop as a result of the conflict, climax, and resolution?

- ✓ Do the characters' problems reach a resolution? How?

- ✓ How does the resolution affect the characters?

Please note that excerpts and passages in the StudySync® library and this workbook are intended as touchstones to generate interest in an author's work. The excerpts and passages do not substitute for the reading of entire texts, and StudySync® strongly recommends that students seek out and purchase the whole literary or informational work in order to experience it as the author intended. Links to online resellers are available in our digital library. In addition, complete works may be ordered through an authorized reseller by filling out and returning to StudySync® the order form enclosed in this workbook.

Reading & Writing
Companion

19

Skill:
Character

Reread paragraphs 37–42 of "Rikki-Tikki-Tavi." Then, using the Checklist on the previous page, answer the multiple-choice questions below.

⟳ YOUR TURN

1. How does the mother's love for her son affect her actions in paragraph 37?

   ○ A. It prompts her to keep her son away from Rikki-tikki.
   ○ B. It causes a disagreement between her and her husband.
   ○ C. It makes her show affection towards Rikki-tikki.
   ○ D. It makes Rikki-tikki feel nervous staying with the family.

2. What does the dialogue in paragraph 40 suggest about Chuchundra?

   ○ A. He is afraid.
   ○ B. He is easily fooled.
   ○ C. He is optimistic.
   ○ D. He loves Rikki-tikki.

3. Which paragraph shows that Teddy looks to Rikki-tikki for protection?

   ○ A. 37
   ○ B. 38
   ○ C. 39
   ○ D. 40

Close Read

RIKKI-TIKKI-TAVI
studysync®

Reread "Rikki-Tikki-Tavi." As you reread, complete the Skills Focus questions below. Then use your answers and annotations from the questions to help you complete the Write activity.

◎ SKILLS FOCUS

1. Identify details that reveal Nag's character when he is first introduced in the story. Explain what inferences you can make about Nag and what makes him a threat.

2. Identify details that reveal Rikki-tikki's character traits as a fighter. Explain how those character traits help Rikki-tikki defeat the snakes.

3. Find examples of Nag and Nagaina's actions and dialogue. How do their words and behaviors create conflict in the plot?

4. Identify details that help you compare and contrast Rikki-tikki and Darzee. Explain what you can infer about Rikki-tikki and Darzee from these details.

5. Analyze details that show how Rikki-tikki beats the snakes. Explain Rikki-tikki's approach to conflict.

✏ WRITE

LITERARY ANALYSIS: In this classic story of good vs. evil, Nag and Nagaina are portrayed as the villains. Consider the role and behaviors of the typical villain. Then think about Nag and Nagaina's behaviors, including how they impact the plot and interact with other characters. Do you think that Nag and Nagaina are truly evil, or have they been unfairly cast as villains? Choose a side, and write a brief response explaining your position and analysis. Use several pieces of textual evidence to support your points.

The Wise Old Woman

FICTION
Yoshiko Uchida
1965

Introduction

"The Wise Old Woman" is a traditional Japanese folktale retold by Yoshiko Uchida (1921–1992), a Japanese American author who grew up in California during the Great Depression. As a child, Uchida's parents taught her to appreciate the customs and folktales of their native land, and as a result, Japanese culture is prevalent in Uchida's writing. Through her writing, Uchida expressed the hope that "all children, in whatever country they may live, have the same love of fun and a good story."

"On and on he climbed, not wanting to stop and leave her behind."

1 Many long years ago, there lived an **arrogant** and cruel young lord who ruled over a small village in the western hills of Japan.

2 "I have no use for old people in my village," he said haughtily. "They are neither useful nor able to work for a living. I therefore **decree** that anyone over seventy-one must be **banished** from the village and left in the mountains to die."

3 "What a dreadful decree! What a cruel and unreasonable lord we have," the people of the village murmured. But the lord fearfully punished anyone who disobeyed him, and so villagers who turned seventy-one were tearfully carried into the mountains, never to return.

4 Gradually there were fewer and fewer old people in the village and soon they disappeared altogether. Then the young lord was pleased.

5 "What a fine village of young, healthy, and hard-working people I have," he bragged. "Soon it will be the finest village in all of Japan."

6 Now, there lived in this village a kind young farmer and his aged mother. They were poor, but the farmer was good to his mother, and the two of them lived happily together. However, as the years went by, the mother grew older, and before long she reached the terrible age of seventy-one.

7 "If only I could somehow **deceive** the cruel lord," the farmer thought. But there were records in the village books and everyone knew that his mother had turned seventy-one.

8 Each day the son put off telling his mother that he must take her into the mountains to die, but the people of the village began to talk. The farmer knew that if he did not take his mother away soon, the lord would send his soldiers and throw them both into a dark dungeon to die a terrible death.

9 "Mother—" he would begin, as he tried to tell her what he must do, but he could not go on.

10 Then one day the mother herself spoke of the lord's dreaded decree. "Well, my son," she said, "the time has come for you to take me to the mountains.

Skill:
Summarizing

- **Who?** the young lord
- **What?** banishes all of the old people to the mountains
- **Where?** the village
- **When?** once the villagers are over the age of seventy-one
- **Why?** He doesn't believe old people are useful or can work.
- **How?** using his power as the ruler of the village

We must hurry before the lord sends his soldiers for you." And she did not seem worried at all that she must go to the mountains to die.

11　"Forgive me, dear mother, for what I must do," the farmer said sadly, and the next morning he lifted his mother to his shoulders and set off on the steep path toward the mountains. Up and up he climbed, until the trees clustered close and the path was gone. There was no longer even the sound of birds, and they heard only the soft wail of the wind in the trees. The son walked slowly, for he could not bear to think of leaving his old mother in the mountains. On and on he climbed, not wanting to stop and leave her behind. Soon, he heard his mother breaking off small twigs from the trees that they passed.

12　"Mother, what are you doing?" he asked.

13　"Do not worry, my son," she answered gently. "I am just marking the way so you will not get lost returning to the village."

14　The son stopped. "Even now you are thinking of me?" he asked, wonderingly.

15　The mother nodded. "Of course, my son," she replied. "You will always be in my thoughts. How could it be otherwise?"

16　At that, the young farmer could bear it no longer. "Mother, I cannot leave you in the mountains to die all alone," he said. "We are going home and no matter what the lord does to punish me, I will never desert you again."

17　So they waited until the sun had set and a lone star crept into the silent sky. Then, in the dark shadows of night, the farmer carried his mother down the hill and they returned quietly to their little house. The farmer dug a deep hole in the floor of his kitchen and made a small room where he could hide his mother. From that day, she spent all her time in the secret room and the farmer carried meals to her there. The rest of the time, he was careful to work in the fields and act as though he lived alone. In this way, for almost two years he kept his mother safely hidden and no one in the village knew that she was there.

18　Then one day there was a terrible **commotion** among the villagers, for Lord Higa of the town beyond the hills threatened to conquer their village and make it his own.

19　"Only one thing can spare you," Lord Higa announced. "Bring me a box containing one thousand ropes of ash and I will spare your village."

20　The cruel young lord quickly gathered together all the wise men of his village. "You are men of wisdom," he said. "Surely you can tell me how to meet Lord Higa's demands so our village can be spared."

21　But the wise men shook their heads. "It is impossible to make even one rope of ash, sire," they answered. "How can we ever make one thousand?"

22   "Fools!" the lord cried angrily. "What good is your wisdom if you cannot help me now?"

23   And he posted a notice in the village square offering a great reward of gold to any villager who could help him save their village.

24   But all the people in the village whispered, "Surely, it is an impossible thing, for ash crumbles at the touch of the finger. How could anyone ever make a rope of ash?" They shook their heads and sighed, "Alas, alas, we must be conquered by yet another cruel lord."

25   The young farmer, too, supposed that this must be, and he wondered what would happen to his mother if a new lord even more terrible than their own came to rule over them.

26   When his mother saw the troubled look on his face, she asked, "Why are you so worried, my son?"

27   So the farmer told her of the impossible demand made by Lord Higa if the village was to be spared, but his mother did not seem troubled at all. Instead she laughed softly and said, "Why, that is not such an impossible task. All one has to do is soak ordinary rope in salt water and dry it well. When it is burned, it will hold its shape and there is your rope of ash! Tell the villagers to hurry and find one thousand pieces of rope."

28   The farmer shook his head in amazement. "Mother, you are wonderfully wise," he said, and he rushed to tell the young lord what he must do.

29   "You are wiser than all the wise men of the village," the lord said when he heard the farmer's solution, and he rewarded him with many pieces of gold. The thousand ropes of ash were quickly made and the village was spared.

30   In a few days, however, there was another great commotion in the village as Lord Higa sent another threat. This time he sent a log with a small hole that curved and bent seven times through its length, and he demanded that a single piece of silk thread be threaded through the hole. "If you cannot perform this task," the lord threatened, "I shall come to conquer your village."

31   The young lord hurried once more to his wise men, but they all shook their heads in bewilderment. "A needle cannot bend its way through such curves," they moaned. "Again we are faced with an impossible demand."

32   "And again you are stupid fools!" the lord said, stamping his foot impatiently. He then posted a second notice in the village square asking the villagers for their help.

33   Once more the young farmer hurried with the problem to his mother in her secret room.

Skill:
Theme

The farmer and the people in the village thought Lord Higa's task was impossible. The mother laughed at the task because she knew it was not impossible. She gave great advice!

This dialogue makes me think the theme might be old people are wise.

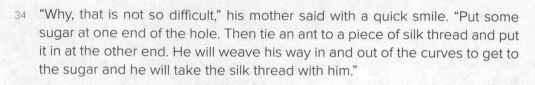

34   "Why, that is not so difficult," his mother said with a quick smile. "Put some sugar at one end of the hole. Then tie an ant to a piece of silk thread and put it in at the other end. He will weave his way in and out of the curves to get to the sugar and he will take the silk thread with him."

35   "Mother, you are remarkable!" the son cried, and he hurried off to the lord with the solution to the second problem.

36   Once more the lord **commended** the young farmer and rewarded him with many pieces of gold. "You are a brilliant man and you have saved our village again," he said gratefully.

37   But the lord's troubles were not over even then, for a few days later Lord Higa sent still another demand. "This time you will undoubtedly fail and then I shall conquer your village," he threatened. "Bring me a drum that sounds without being beaten."

38   "But that is not possible," sighed the people of the village. "How can anyone make a drum sound without beating it?"

39   This time the wise men held their heads in their hands and moaned, "It is hopeless. It is hopeless. This time Lord Higa will conquer us all."

40   The young farmer hurried home breathlessly. "Mother, Mother, we must solve another terrible problem or Lord Higa will conquer our village!" And he quickly told his mother about the impossible drum.

41   His mother, however, smiled and answered, "Why, this is the easiest of them all. Make a drum with sides of paper and put a bumblebee inside. As it tries to escape, it will buzz and beat itself against the paper and you will have a drum that sounds without being beaten."

42   The young farmer was amazed at his mother's wisdom. "You are far wiser than any of the wise men of the village," he said, and he hurried to tell the young lord how to meet Lord Higa's third demand.

43   When the lord heard the answer, he was greatly impressed. "Surely a young man like you cannot be wiser than all my wise men," he said. "Tell me honestly, who has helped you solve all these difficult problems?"

44   The young farmer could not lie. "My lord," he began slowly, "for the past two years I have broken the law of the land. I have kept my aged mother hidden beneath the floor of my house, and it is she who solved each of your problems and saved the village from Lord Higa."

45   He trembled as he spoke, for he feared the lord's displeasure and rage. Surely now the soldiers would be summoned to throw him into the dark dungeon. But when he glanced fearfully at the lord, he saw that the young

ruler was not angry at all. Instead, he was silent and thoughtful, for at last he realized how much wisdom and knowledge old people possess.

46 "I have been very wrong," he said finally. "And I must ask the forgiveness of your mother and of all my people. Never again will I demand that the old people of our village be sent to the mountains to die. Rather, they will be treated with the respect and honor they deserve and share with us the wisdom of their years."

47 And so it was. From that day, the villagers were no longer forced to abandon their parents in the mountains, and the village became once more a happy, cheerful place in which to live. The terrible Lord Higa stopped sending his impossible demands and no longer threatened to conquer them, for he too was impressed.

48 "Even in such a small village there is much wisdom," he declared, "and its people should be allowed to live in peace."

49 And that is exactly what the farmer and his mother and all the people of the village did for all the years thereafter.

Please note that excerpts and passages in the StudySync® library and this workbook are intended as touchstones to generate interest in an author's work. The excerpts and passages do not substitute for the reading of entire texts, and StudySync® strongly recommends that students seek out and purchase the whole literary or informational work in order to experience it as the author intended. Links to online resellers are available in our digital library. In addition, complete works may be ordered through an authorized reseller by filling out and returning to StudySync® the order form enclosed in this workbook.

Reading & Writing Companion   27

First Read

Read "The Wise Old Woman." After you read, complete the Think Questions below.

☁ THINK QUESTIONS

1. Why did the young lord issue a decree against elderly people? What did the decree say? Cite specific evidence from the second paragraph.

2. Write two to three sentences describing how the farmer's mother saves the village from Lord Higa's threats. Be sure to use evidence from the text in your response.

3. How does the young lord change at the end of the story? What causes this change? Use evidence from the text to support your answer.

4. Use context clues to determine the meaning of **commended** as it is used in paragraph 36 of "The Wise Old Woman." Write your definition here and identify clues that helped you figure out the meaning. Then check the meaning in a dictionary.

5. Find the word **banished** in paragraph 2 of "The Wise Old Woman." Use context clues in the surrounding sentences, as well as the sentence in which the word appears, to determine the word's meaning. Write your definition here and identify clues that helped you figure out its meaning.

Skill:
Summarizing

Use the Checklist to analyze Summarizing in "The Wise Old Woman." Refer to the sample student annotations about Summarizing in the text.

••• CHECKLIST FOR SUMMARIZING

In order to provide an objective summary of a text, note the following:

- ✓ answers to the basic questions *who*, *what*, *where*, *when*, *why*, and *how*

- ✓ when summarizing literature, note the setting, characters, and major events in the plot, including the problem the characters face and how it is solved

- ✓ stay objective, and do not add your own personal thoughts, judgments, or opinions to the summary

To provide an objective summary of a text, consider the following questions:

- ✓ What are the answers to basic *who*, *what*, *where*, *when*, *why*, and *how* questions?

- ✓ Is my summary objective, or have I added my own thoughts, judgments, and personal opinions?

Skill:
Summarizing

Reread paragraphs 6–11 of "The Wise Old Woman." Then, complete the chart by matching the important details with each category to objectively summarize what happened in the text.

⟳ YOUR TURN

	Important Detail Options
A	The farmer kept putting off telling his mother it was time to go to the mountains to die.
B	years after the decree
C	the young farmer and the aged mother
D	a village in Japan
E	with sadness
F	The farmer cared for his mother and did not want her to die.

Who	What	Where	When	Why	How

Reading & Writing Companion

Skill:
Theme

Use the Checklist to analyze Theme in "The Wise Old Woman." Refer to the sample student annotations about Theme in the text.

••• CHECKLIST FOR THEME

In order to identify a theme in a text, note the following:

- ✓ the topic of the text

- ✓ whether or not the theme is stated directly in the text

- ✓ details in the text that help to reveal theme

  - • a narrator's or speaker's tone

  - • title and chapter headings

  - • details about the setting

  - • characters' thoughts, actions, and dialogue

  - • the central conflict in the story's plot

  - • the resolution of the conflict

To determine a theme of a text and analyze its development over the course of the text, consider the following questions:

- ✓ What is a theme of the text?

- ✓ When did you become aware of that theme? For instance, did the story's conclusion reveal the theme?

- ✓ How does the theme develop over the course of the text?

Please note that excerpts and passages in the StudySync® library and this workbook are intended as touchstones to generate interest in an author's work. The excerpts and passages do not substitute for the reading of entire texts, and StudySync® strongly recommends that students seek out and purchase the whole literary or informational work in order to experience it as the author intended. Links to online resellers are available in our digital library. In addition, complete works may be ordered through an authorized reseller by filling out and returning to StudySync® the order form enclosed in this workbook.

Reading & Writing
Companion

31

Skill:
Theme

Reread paragraphs 40–46 of "The Wise Old Woman." Then, using the Checklist on the previous page, answer the multiple-choice questions below.

🔄 YOUR TURN

1. The change the young lord undergoes in paragraph 45 suggests a theme about which topic?

   ○ A. Hope
   ○ B. Change
   ○ C. Humility
   ○ D. Fear

2. Identify the theme that best matches the young lord's change in paragraph 46.

   ○ A. Being a good ruler means being willing to accept when you are wrong and change your behavior.
   ○ B. Being a good ruler means being able to get people to comply with your wishes and demands.
   ○ C. People will do good work only when they are afraid.
   ○ D. Love is a stronger motivator to get work done than fear.

Close Read

Reread "The Wise Old Woman." As you reread, complete the Skills Focus questions below. Then use your answers and annotations from the questions to help you complete the Write activity.

◎ SKILLS FOCUS

1. Reread the beginning of the story, including scenes that describe how the young farmer hides and cares for his mother. Highlight and annotate important details that you would include in a summary. What topics or themes are suggested by these details?

2. Identify scenes that reveal the character traits of the farmer's mother. Explain how her character traits influence the events in the story.

3. Identify evidence that shows how the farmer's mother helped the village avoid conflict. How do her actions contribute to the development of the theme?

✏ WRITE

LITERARY ANALYSIS: Provide a brief objective summary of the story, including only the most important details from the beginning, middle, and end. Then think about how the farmer's mother relies on her son. Think about how the village and the young lord rely on the farmer's mother. What theme is developed through these relationships and the story's resolution? Use several pieces of textual evidence to support your analysis.

Woodsong

INFORMATIONAL TEXT
Gary Paulsen
1990

Introduction

I n his memoir, *Woodsong*, the esteemed outdoorsman, former beaver trapper, and three-time Newbery Honor author Gary Paulsen (b. 1939) tells the story of his interconnected life with nature. From employment-requisite dog sledding in Minnesota, to the thousand-mile race from Settler's Bay to Nome, Alaska, Paulsen's tales usually come down to the bare-bone realities of survival—be it putting food on his family's table or avoiding being dinner for something else. In this excerpt from the first chapter, Paulsen learns a valuable lesson from the wild and often brutal laws of the forest.

"In all my time in the woods, in the wondrous dance of it, I have many times seen predators fail."

from Chapter One

1   I lived in innocence for a long time. I believed in the fairy-tale version of the forest until I was close to forty years old.

2   **Gulled** by Disney and others, I believed Bambi always got out of the fire. Nothing ever really got hurt. Though I hunted and killed it was always somehow clean and removed from reality. I killed yet thought that every story had a happy ending.

3   Until a December morning . . .

4   I was running a dog team around the side of a large lake, just starting out on my trapline[1]. It was early winter and the ice on the lake wasn't thick enough to support the sled and team or I would have gone across the middle. There was a rough trail around the edge of the lake and I was running a fresh eight-dog team so the small loop, which added five or so miles, presented no great difficulty.

5   It was a grandly beautiful winter morning. The temperature was perhaps ten below, with a bright sun that shone through ice crystals in the air so that everything seemed to sparkle. The dogs were working evenly, the gangline[2] up through the middle of them thrumming with the rhythm it has when they are working in perfect **tandem**. We skirted the lake, which lay below and to the right. To the left and rising higher were willows and brush, which made something like a wall next to the trail.

6   The dogs were still running at a lope, though we had come over seven miles, and I was full of them; my life was full of them. We were, as it happens sometimes, dancing with winter. I could not help smiling, just smiling idiotically at the grandness of it. Part of the chant of an ancient Navajo prayer rolled through my mind:

7   *Beauty above me*
Beauty below me
Beauty before me. . .

---

1. **trapline**   a route along which traps are set for wild animals or other game
2. **gangline**   the central line in front of a sled to which each individual animal is attached

---

NOTES

Skill:
Connotation and Denotation

This is an important description of the setting. The dictionary definition of fairy tale is "a magical story." This creates a positive emotion because fairy tales are usually happy. The author had a good feeling about the forest.

8 That is how I felt then and frequently still feel when I am running dogs. I was in and of beauty and at that **precise** moment a doe, a white-tailed deer, exploded out of some willows on the left side of the team, heading down the bank toward the lake.

9 The snow alongside the trail was about two feet deep and powdery and it followed her in a white shower that covered everything. She literally flew over the lead dog who was a big, white, wolfy-looking male named Dollar. He was so surprised that he dropped, ducked, for part of an instant, then rose—almost like a rock skipping on the trail—and continued running. We were moving so fast and the deer was moving so fast that within a second or two we were several yards past where it happened and yet everything seemed suspended in slow motion.

10 Above all, in the deer, was the stink of fear. Even in that split part of a second, it could be smelled. It could be seen. The doe's eyes were so wide they seemed to come out of her head. Her mouth was jacked open and her tongue hung out to the side. Her jaw and neck were covered with spit, and she stunk of fear.

**Skill:
Connotation and Denotation**

The dictionary definition of stink is "an unpleasant smell," which has negative connotations. Using this phrase rather than saying the doe "smelled" of fear emphasizes just how terrified the deer is as she runs from the wolves.

11 Dogs smell fear at once but I have not always been able to, even when I was afraid. There is something coppery about it, a metallic smell mixed with the smell of urine and feces, when something, when somebody, is afraid. No, not just afraid but ripped with fear, and it was on the doe.

12 The smell excited the dogs and they began to run faster, although continuing down the trail; I turned to look back from the sled and saw why the doe was frightened.

13 Wolves.

14 They bounded over the trail after the doe even as I watched. These were not the large timber wolves but the smaller northern brush wolves, perhaps weighing forty or fifty pounds each, about as large as most of my team. I think they are called northern coyotes.

15 Except that they act as wolves. They pack and have pack social structures like timber wolves, and hunt in packs like timber wolves.

16 And they were hunting the doe.

17 There were seven of them and not one looked down the trail to see me as they jumped across the sled tracks after the deer. They were so **intent** on her, and the smell of her, that I might as well not have existed.

18 And they were gaining on her.

19 I stood on the brakes to stop the sled and set the snow-hook to hold the dogs and turned. The dogs immediately swung down off the trail toward the lake, trying to get at the wolves and deer. The snowhook came loose and we began to slide down the lake bank. I jerked the hook from the snow and hooked it on a small poplar that held us.

20 The doe, in horror now, and knowing what was coming, left the bank of the lake and bounded out onto the bad ice. Her tail was fully erect, a white flash as she tried to reach out and get speed, but the ice was too thin.

21 Too thin for all the weight of her on the small, pointed hooves and she went through and down in a huge spray of shattered ice and water.

22 She was up instantly, clambering and working to get back up on top of the ice next to the hole. Through sheer effort in her panic she made it.

23 But it slowed her too much.

24 In those few moments of going through the ice and getting out she lost her lead on the wolves and they were on her.

25 On her.

26 In all my time in the woods, in the wondrous dance of it, I have many times seen predators fail. As a matter of fact, they usually fail. I once saw a beaver come out of a hole on the ice near his lodge in the middle of winter and stand off four wolves. He **sustained** one small bite on his tail and **inflicted** terrible damage with his teeth on the wolves, killing one and wounding the other three. I have seen rabbits outwit foxes and watched red squirrels tease martens and get away with it, but this time it was not to be.

Excerpted from *Woodsong* by Gary Paulsen, published by Simon & Schuster.

 Skill: Author's Purpose and Point of View

The author describes his time in the woods as a "wondrous dance." He has seen rabbits outwit foxes. This may be why he thought nothing ever got hurt. But "this time it was not to be." The death of the doe changes the author's point of view.

WOODSONG

First Read

Read *Woodsong*. After you read, complete the Think Questions below.

1. What does the reader learn about the ice in paragraph 4? How does this information prepare the reader for what happens later in the story? Cite textual evidence in your response.

2. Paulsen uses sensory details—words that appeal to the senses of sight, sound, smell, and taste—to describe the feeling of fear. How does Paulsen describe fear and the reaction of his sled dogs to fear? Refer to the text in your answer.

3. In the final paragraph, Paulsen shares an example of another animal battle. What is that example? How is it different from the story of the wolves and the doe?

4. Find the word **tandem** in paragraph 5 of *Woodsong*. Use context clues in the surrounding sentences, as well as the sentence in which the word appears, to determine the word's meaning. Write your definition here and identify clues that helped you figure out its meaning.

5. Use context clues to determine the meaning of **inflicted** as it is used in last paragraph of *Woodsong*. Write your definition here and identify clues that helped you figure out the meaning. Then check the meaning in a dictionary.

Skill: Connotation and Denotation

Use the Checklist to analyze Connotation and Denotation in *Woodsong*. Refer to the sample student annotations about Connotation and Denotation in the text.

••• CHECKLIST FOR CONNOTATION AND DENOTATION

In order to identify the connotative meanings of words, use the following steps:

✓ First, note unfamiliar words and phrases, key words used to describe important events and ideas, or words that inspire an emotional reaction.

✓ Next, determine and note the denotative meaning of words by consulting reference materials such as a dictionary, a glossary, or a thesaurus.

To better understand the meanings of words and phrases as they are used in the text, including connotative meanings, use the following questions:

✓ What is the genre or subject of the text? How does that affect the possible meaning of a word or phrase?

✓ Does the word create positive, negative, or neutral emotion?

✓ What synonyms or alternative phrasing help you describe the connotative meaning of the word?

To analyze the impact of word choice on the meaning of a text, use the following questions as a guide:

✓ What is the meaning of the word or phrase? What is the connotation as well as the denotation?

✓ If I substitute a synonym based on denotation, is the meaning the same? How does the synonym change the meaning of the text?

Please note that excerpts and passages in the StudySync® library and this workbook are intended as touchstones to generate interest in an author's work. The excerpts and passages do not substitute for the reading of entire texts, and StudySync® strongly recommends that students seek out and purchase the whole literary or informational work in order to experience it as the author intended. Links to online resellers are available in our digital library. In addition, complete works may be ordered through an authorized reseller by filling out and returning to StudySync® the order form enclosed in this workbook.

Reading & Writing Companion

39

Skill: Connotation and Denotation

Reread paragraphs 10–13 of *Woodsong*. Then, using the Checklist on the previous page, answer the multiple-choice questions below.

⟳ YOUR TURN

1. This question has two parts. First, answer Part A. Then, answer Part B.

   Part A: Which answer best describes the connotation of the word *jacked* as it is used in the first paragraph?

   ○ A. open

   ○ B. terrified

   ○ C. strong

   ○ D. surprised

   Part B: Which line from the passage supports your answer in Part A?

   ○ A. The smell excited the dogs and they began to run faster, although continuing down the trail.

   ○ B. Dogs smell fear at once but I have not always been able to, even when I was afraid.

   ○ C. Above all, in the deer, was the stink of fear. Even in that split part of a second, it could be smelled. It could be seen.

   ○ D. Her jaw and neck were covered with spit, and she stunk of fear.

Skill: Author's Purpose and Point of View

Use the Checklist to analyze Author's Purpose and Point of View in *Woodsong*. Refer to the sample student annotations about Author's Purpose and Point of View in the text.

••• CHECKLIST FOR AUTHOR'S PURPOSE AND POINT OF VIEW

In order to identify author's purpose and point of view, note the following:

✓ facts, statistics, and graphic aids, as these indicate that an author is writing to inform.

✓ descriptive or sensory details and emotional language that may indicate that an author is writing to describe and dramatize events.

✓ descriptions that present a complicated process in plain language may indicate that an author is writing to explain.

✓ emotional language with a call to action may indicate the author is trying to persuade readers or stress an opinion.

✓ the language the author uses can also be a clue to the author's point of view on a subject or topic.

To determine the author's purpose and point of view in a text, consider the following questions:

✓ How does the author convey, or communicate, information in the text?

✓ Does the author use figurative or emotional language? How does it affect the purpose and point of view?

✓ Are charts, graphs, maps and other graphic aids included in the text? For what purpose?

AUTHOR'S PURPOSE AND
AUTHOR'S POINT OF VIEW

sync•skills

Skill: Author's Purpose and Point of View

Reread paragraphs 5–8 of *Woodsong*. Then, using the Checklist on the previous page, answer the multiple-choice questions below.

♻ YOUR TURN

1. The author's purpose in using many descriptive and sensory details is to —

   ○ A. describe the scene that morning.
   ○ B. persuade the reader that the outdoors should be enjoyed.
   ○ C. entertain the reader with a scene from nature.
   ○ D. criticize commonly held beliefs about nature.

2. Based on the author's descriptions in paragraphs 5–8, the reader can conclude that he primarily wants to express a feeling of —

   ○ A. kinship with the Navajo.
   ○ B. fatigue from leading the dog sled.
   ○ C. anxiety about danger out in the woods.
   ○ D. appreciation for the beauty of nature.

3. Based on the details in the excerpt, the reader can infer that the author's overall purpose in writing this piece is to show that

   ○ A. When you spend time in nature, you can feel the frightening power of the wilderness.
   ○ B. You should not travel or work alone in nature, unless you have a pack of animals with you.
   ○ C. In certain moments you can feel surrounded by beauty in nature, but there is also danger in the natural world.
   ○ D. Reflecting on Native American literature and customs can enhance your appreciation of nature.

WOODSONG

Close Read

Reread *Woodsong*. As you reread, complete the Skills Focus questions below. Then use your answers and annotations from the questions to help you complete the Write activity.

⦿ SKILLS FOCUS

1. Identify details and language used to describe the doe and the wolves. Explain how these details reflect the author's purpose or point of view.

2. Reread paragraphs 5–8. Identify words with specific emotional connotations. Explain why you think the author chose those words.

3. Reread the last paragraph. Identify details that suggest how the author's point of view has changed. Explain how being an outside observer of a conflict between animals affects the author personally.

✎ WRITE

LITERARY ANALYSIS: In this excerpt from his memoir, Gary Paulsen describes wolves attacking and dominating a doe in the forest. Why did Paulsen write about this experience? How did the experience change him? Use textual evidence to answer these questions. In your response, explain how Paulsen uses words with strong connotative meanings and other descriptive details to convey his purpose and point of view.

Nimona

FICTION
Noelle Stevenson
2015

Introduction

Comic artist and illustrator Noelle Stevenson (b. 1991) was a National Book Award finalist for her critically acclaimed and groundbreaking graphic novel *Nimona*, an irreverent take on the traditional medieval fantasy narrative. Nimona is the brazen young sidekick to mad scientist and super villain Lord Ballister Blackheart. In this chapter, Nimona and her boss brainstorm ideas on how to best rid themselves of Blackheart's archnemesis, local hero Sir Goldenloin. *Nimona* was first published in 2015.

"You can't just go around murdering people. There are RULES, Nimona."

NOTES

Skill:
Textual Evidence

Blackheart says, "If anyone is going to kill him ... it's going to be me." The color fades and I see a young Blackheart in a flashback. I can infer that Sir Goldenloin and Blackheart must have a complicated past.

First Read

Read *Nimona*. After you read, complete the Think Questions below.

1. What are three differences between Blackheart's and Nimona's plans to attack the city? Support your answer using details from the text.

2. Using details from the text, summarize the feud between Blackheart and Sir Goldenloin.

3. How is Nimona's definition of what it means to be a villain different from Blackheart's definition? Support your answer using details from the text.

4. Find the word **emphasis** in panel 6 on page 45 of *Nimona*. Use context clues in the surrounding sentences, as well as the sentence in which the word appears, to determine the word's meaning. Write your definition here and identify clues that helped you figure out its meaning.

5. Use context clues to determine the meaning of **pitted** as it is used in panel 21 on page 47 of *Nimona*. Write your definition here and identify clues that helped you figure out its meaning. Then check the meaning in a dictionary.

Please note that excerpts and passages in the StudySync® library and this workbook are intended as touchstones to generate interest in an author's work. The excerpts and passages do not substitute for the reading of entire texts, and StudySync® strongly recommends that students seek out and purchase the whole literary or informational work in order to experience it as the author intended. Links to online resellers are available in our digital library. In addition, complete works may be ordered through an authorized reseller by filling out and returning to StudySync® the order form enclosed in this workbook.

Reading & Writing Companion   49

Skill:
Textual Evidence

Use the Checklist to analyze Textual Evidence in *Nimona*. Refer to the sample student annotations about Textual Evidence in the text.

••• CHECKLIST FOR TEXTUAL EVIDENCE

In order to support an inference by citing evidence that is explicitly stated in the text, do the following:

✓ read the text closely and critically

✓ identify what the text says explicitly

✓ find the most relevant textual evidence that supports your analysis

✓ consider why an author explicitly states specific details and information

✓ cite the specific words, phrases, sentences, paragraphs, or images from the text that support your analysis

In order to interpret implicit meanings in a text by making inferences, do the following:

✓ combine information directly stated in the text with your own knowledge, experiences, and observations

✓ cite the specific words, phrases, sentences, paragraphs, or images from the text that support this inference

In order to cite textual evidence to support an analysis of what the text says explicitly as well as inferences drawn from the text, consider the following questions:

✓ Have I read the text closely and critically?

✓ What inferences am I making about the text? What textual evidence am I using to support these inferences?

✓ Am I quoting the evidence from the text correctly?

✓ Does my textual evidence logically relate to my analysis?

✓ Have I cited several pieces of textual evidence?

Skill:
Textual Evidence

sync•skills

Complete the chart below by matching the correct background knowledge and implicit meaning with each explicit meaning.

⟳ YOUR TURN

	Background Knowledge and Implicit Meaning Options
A	I know that to get into a special school like the Hero Institution, you have to be one of the best for your age.
B	I know that knights wear armor.
C	A change in Sir Goldenloin's feelings toward Blackheart occurred when they had to compete against each other.
D	Blackheart and Sir Goldenloin appeared to be equally the best.
E	I know that sometimes when friends compete, their friendship can change.
F	Both Blackheart and Sir Goldenloin were young, brave knights.

Explicit Evidence	Background Knowledge	Implicit Meaning
Blackheart and Sir Goldenloin were "heroes in training." They both wear armor in the image.		
Blackheart and Sir Goldenloin were "the two most promising heroes the Institution had ever seen." They are standing next to each other in the image.		
Blackheart and Sir Goldenloin were friends "until the day of the joust." Sir Goldenloin's arm is down while Blackheart's arm is on Goldenloin's back in the image.		

Please note that excerpts and passages in the StudySync® library and this workbook are intended as touchstones to generate interest in an author's work. The excerpts and passages do not substitute for the reading of entire texts, and StudySync® strongly recommends that students seek out and purchase the whole literary or informational work in order to experience it as the author intended. Links to online resellers are available in our digital library. In addition, complete works may be ordered through an authorized reseller by filling out and returning to StudySync® the order form enclosed in this workbook.

Reading & Writing
Companion

51

Close Read

Reread *Nimona*. As you reread, complete the Skills Focus questions below. Then use your answers and annotations from the questions to help you complete the Write activity.

◎ SKILLS FOCUS

1. How would you describe Nimona? Cite the specific words, phrases, sentences, or images from the text to support your analysis and inferences.

2. Identify parts in the flashback that help you empathize with Blackheart. Explain what the flashback makes you think and feel about Blackheart.

3. Identify details that you can use to compare and contrast the characters of Nimona and Blackheart. Explain how the two characters are different and similar. Consider how each character responds to plot events.

4. Explain the difference in how Sir Blackheart and Nimona approach conflict. Cite textual evidence to support your response.

✎ WRITE

DEBATE PLAN: Imagine that you are either Nimona or Blackheart. As Nimona, you want to convince Blackheart to adopt your changes to his evil plan. As Blackheart, you want to ensure that Nimona follows your rules of battle. Choose the persona of either Nimona or Blackheart and prepare points for a debate to convince the other character to fight according to your style. Use several pieces of textual evidence to support your argument and any counter-arguments. Be sure to consider what the text says explicitly and your own inferences about the characters.

Stargirl

FICTION
Jerry Spinelli
2000

Introduction

Stargirl is an homage to individuality and self-confidence by Jerry Spinelli (b. 1941), an American author of award-winning children's and young adult fiction. The novel and its sequel, *Love, Stargirl*, have inspired many students to start their own "Stargirl Societies" in schools around the country. When Stargirl first shows up at Mica Area High School, narrator Leo and the other students don't know what to make of her. She acts and dresses differently from everyone else. She doesn't try to fit in; instead, she stands out. Stargirl's antics have everyone convinced that she cannot be real—or is she?

"How long do you think somebody who's *really* like that is going to last around here?"

from Chapter 2

1   I had to admit, the more I saw of her, the easier it was to believe she was a plant, a joke, anything but real. On that second day she wore bright-red baggy shorts with a bib and shoulder straps—overall shorts. Her sandy hair was pulled back into twin plaited pigtails, each tied with a bright-red ribbon. A rouge smudge applied each cheek, and she had even dabbed some oversized freckles on her face. She looked like Heidi. Or Bo Peep.

2   At lunch she was alone again at her table. As before, when she finished eating, she took up her ukulele. But this time she didn't play. She got up and started walking among the tables. She stared at us. She stared at one face, then another and another. The kind of bold, I'm looking at you stare you almost never get from people, especially strangers. She appeared to be looking for someone, and the whole lunchroom had become very uncomfortable.

3   As she approached our table, I thought: *What if she's looking for me?* The thought terrified me. So I turned from her. I looked at Kevin. I watched him grin goofily up at her. He wiggled his fingers at her and whispered, "Hi, Stargirl." I didn't hear an answer. I was **intensely** aware of her passing behind my chair.

4   She stopped two tables away. She was smiling at a pudding-bodied senior named Alan Ferko. The lunchroom was dead silent. She started strumming the uke. And singing. It was "Happy Birthday." When she came to his name she didn't just sing his first name, but his full name:

5   "Happy Birthday, dear Alan Fer-kooooh"

6   Alan Ferko's face turned red as Bo Peep's pigtail ribbons. There was a flurry of whistles and hoots, more for Alan Ferko's sake, I think, than hers. As Stargirl marched out, I could see Hillari Kimble across the lunchroom rising from her seat, pointing, saying something I could not hear.

7   "I'll tell you one thing," Kevin said as we joined the mob in the hallways, "she better be fake."

NOTES

8   I asked him what he meant.

9   "I mean if she's real, she's in big trouble. How long do you think somebody who's *really* like that is going to last around here?"

10   Good question.

11   Mica Area High School—MAHS—was not exactly a hotbed of **nonconformity.** There were individual **variants** here and there, of course, but within pretty narrow limits we all wore the same clothes, talked the same way, ate the same food, listened to the same music. Even our dorks and nerds had a MAHS stamp on them. If we happened to somehow distinguish ourselves, we quickly snapped back into place, like rubber bands.

12   Kevin was right. It was unthinkable that Stargirl could survive—or at least survive unchanged—among us. But it was also clear that Hillari Kimble was at least half right: this person calling herself Stargirl may or may not have been a faculty plant for school spirit, but whatever she was, she was not real.

13   She couldn't be.

14   Several times in those early weeks of September, she showed up in something outrageous. A 1920s flapper dress. An Indian buckskin. A kimono. One day she wore a denim miniskirt with green stockings, and crawling up one leg was a parade of enamel ladybug and butterfly pins. "Normal" for her were long, floor-brushing pioneer dresses and skirts.

15   Every few days in the lunchroom she serenaded someone new with "Happy Birthday." I was glad my birthday was in the summer.

16   In the hallways, she said hello to perfect strangers. The seniors couldn't believe it. They had never seen a tenth-grader so bold.

17   In class she was always flapping her hand in the air, asking questions, though the question often had nothing to do with the subject. One day she asked a question about trolls—in U.S. History class.

18   She made a song about isosceles triangles. She sang it to her Plane Geometry class. It was called "Three Sides Have I, But Only Two are Equal."

19   She joined the cross-country team. Our house meets were held on the Mica Country Club golf course. Red flags showed the runners the way to go. In her first meet, out in the middle of the course, she turned left when everyone else turned right. They waited for her at the finish line. She never showed up. She was dismissed from the team.

20   One day a girl screamed in the hallway. She had seen a tiny brown face pop up from Stargirl's sunflower canvas bag. It was her pet rat. It rode to school in the bag every day.

21 One morning we had a rare rainfall. It came during her gym class. The teacher told everyone to come in. On the way to the next class they looked out the windows. Stargirl was still outside. In the rain. Dancing.

22 We wanted to **define** her, to wrap her up as we did each other, but we could not seem to get past "weird" and "strange" and "goofy." Her ways knocked us off balance. A single word seemed to hover in the cloudless sky over the school:

23 HUH?

24 Everything she did seemed to echo Hillari Kimble: She's not real... She's not real...

25 And each night in bed I thought of her as the moon came through my window. I could have lowered my shade to make it darker and easier to sleep, but I never did. In that moonlit hour, I **acquired** a sense of the otherness of things. I liked the feeling the moonlight gave me, as if it wasn't the opposite of day, but its underside, its private side, when the fabulous purred on my snow-white sheet like some dark cat come in from the desert.

26 It was during one of these nightmoon times that it came to me that Hillari Kimble was wrong. Stargirl *was* real.

Excerpted from *Stargirl* by Jerry Spinelli, published by Ember Publishing.

✏ WRITE

PERSONAL RESPONSE: Leo states, "If we happened to somehow distinguish ourselves, we quickly snapped back into place, like rubber bands." Explain what Leo means by this observation. How does it apply to him and his classmates? Is it important for individuals to restrict themselves so they can fit in, or should they try to distinguish themselves from others? Make a case for the importance of either conformity or individuality, using Leo's observations of Stargirl.

Seventh Grade

FICTION
Gary Soto
1995

Introduction

Gary Soto (b. 1952) is a Mexican American author born in Fresno, California, at the heart of California's San Joaquin Valley, where Mr. Soto worked as a young man in the area's agricultural fields. It was there he began to reflect on the kinds of stories he wanted to tell. Much of Soto's fiction and poetry focuses on Chicano men and women of all ages, wrapped up in everyday life—and the small moments that reveal the largest truths. This humorous short story, "Seventh Grade," follows young Victor Rodriguez on his first day back at school. As he huddles with his friend Michael about how to impress their female classmates, Victor is struck by his affection for Teresa, leading to both embarrassment and possibility.

"She smiled sweetly and gathered her books. Her next class was French, same as Victor's."

NOTES

1   On the first day of school, Victor stood in line half an hour before he came to a wobbly card table. He was handed a packet of papers and a computer card on which he listed his one elective, French. He already spoke Spanish and English, but he thought some day he might travel to France, where it was cool; not like Fresno, where summer days reached 110 degrees in the shade. There were rivers in France, and huge churches, and fair-skinned people everywhere, the way there were brown people all around Victor.

2   Besides, Teresa, a girl he had liked since they were in catechism classes[1] at Saint Theresa's, was taking French, too. With any luck they would be in the same class. *Teresa is going to be my girl this year,* he promised himself as he left the gym full of students in their new fall clothes. She was cute. And good in math, too, Victor thought as he walked down the hall to his homeroom. He ran into his friend, Michael Torres, by the water fountain that never turned off.

3   They shook hands, *raza*[2]-style, and jerked their heads at one another in a *saludo de vato*[3]. "How come you're making a face?" asked Victor.

4   "I ain't making a face, *ese*. This is my face." Michael said his face had changed during the summer. He had read a GQ magazine that his older brother had borrowed from the Book Mobile and noticed that the male models all had the same look on their faces. They would stand, one arm around a beautiful woman, and **scowl**. They would sit at the pool, their rippled stomachs dark with shadow, and *scowl*. They would sit at dinner tables, cool drinks in their hands, and *scowl*.

5   "I think it works," Michael said. He scowled and let his upper lip quiver. His teeth showed along with the ferocity of his soul. "Belinda Reyes walked by a while ago and looked at me," he said.

6   Victor didn't say anything, though he thought his friend looked pretty strange. They talked about recent movies, baseball, their parents, and the horrors of

---

Skill:
Setting

The story is set in school at the beginning of the year. Students are back in one place after months of being apart. Seventh-graders do all kinds of things to impress their peers on the first day. Victor takes French class to be close to his crush. I bet this setting is going to lead to some excitement or problems for him.

1. **catechism classes** classes that serve as an introduction to the core principles of the Christian religion
2. **raza** (Spanish) a term referring to peoples of Hispanic descent
3. **saludo de vato** (Spanish) an informal greeting (similar to "What's up?")

picking grapes in order to buy their fall clothes. Picking grapes was like living in Siberia, except hot and more boring.

7   "What classes are you taking?" Michael said, scowling.

8   "French. How 'bout you?"

9   "Spanish. I ain't so good at it, even if I'm Mexican."

10   "I'm not either, but I'm better at it than math, that's for sure."

11   A tinny, three-beat bell propelled students to their homerooms. The two friends socked each other in the arm and went their ways, Victor thinking, man, that's weird. Michael thinks making a face makes him handsome.

12   On the way to his homeroom, Victor tried a scowl. He felt foolish, until out of the corner of his eye he saw a girl looking at him. Umm, he thought, maybe it does work. He scowled with greater **conviction.**

13   In the homeroom, roll was taken, emergency cards were passed out, and they were given a bulletin to take home to their parents. The principal, Mr. Belton, spoke over the crackling loudspeaker, welcoming the students to a new year, new experiences, and new friendships. The students squirmed in their chairs and ignored him, they were **anxious** to go to first period. Victor sat calmly, thinking of Teresa, who sat two rows away, reading a paperback novel. This would be his lucky year. She was in his homeroom, and would probably be in his English and math classes. And, of course, French.

14   The bell rang for first period, and the students herded noisily through the door. Only Teresa lingered, talking with the homeroom teacher.

15   "So you think I should talk to Mrs. Gaines?" she asked the teacher. "She would know about ballet?"

16   "She would be a good bet," the teacher said. Then added, "Or the gym teacher, Mrs. Garza."

17   Victor lingered, keeping his head down and staring at his desk. He wanted to leave when she did so he could bump into her and say something clever.

18   He watched her on the sly. As she turned to leave, he stood up and hurried to the door, where he managed to catch her eye. She smiled and said, "Hi, Victor."

19   He smiled back and said, "Yeah, that's me." His brown face blushed. Why hadn't he said, "Hi, Teresa," or "How was your summer?" or something nice?

20   As Teresa walked down the hall, Victor walked the other way, looking back, admiring how gracefully she walked, one foot in front of the other. So much

NOTES

for being in the same class, he thought. As he trudged to English, he practiced scowling.

21 In English they reviewed the parts of speech. Mr. Lucas, a portly man, waddled down the aisle, asking, "What is a noun?"

22 "A person, place, or thing," said the class in **unison.**

23 "Yes, now somebody give me an example of a person—you, Victor Rodriguez."

24 "Teresa," Victor said **automatically.** Some of the girls giggled. They knew he had a crush on Teresa. He felt himself blushing again.

25 "Correct," Mr. Lucas said. "Now provide me with a place."

26 Mr. Lucas called on a freckled kid who answered, "Teresa's house with a kitchen full of big brothers."

27 After English, Victor had math, his weakest subject. He sat in the back by the window, hoping that he would not be called on. Victor understood most of the problems, but some of the stuff looked like the teacher made it up as she went along. It was confusing, like the inside of a watch.

28 After math he had a fifteen-minute break, then social studies, and finally lunch. He bought a tuna casserole with buttered rolls, some fruit cocktail, and milk. He sat with Michael, who practiced scowling between bites.

29 Girls walked by and looked at him, "See what I mean, Vic?" Michael scowled. "They love it."

30 "Yeah, I guess so."

31 They ate slowly, Victor scanning the horizon for a glimpse of Teresa. He didn't see her. She must have brought lunch, he thought, and is eating outside. Victor scraped his plate and left Michael, who was busy scowling at a girl two tables away.

32 The small, triangle-shaped campus bustled with students talking about their new classes. Everyone was in a sunny mood. Victor hurried to the bag lunch area, where he sat down and opened his math book. He moved his lips as if he were reading, but his mind was somewhere else. He raised his eyes slowly and looked around. No Teresa.

33 He lowered his eyes, pretending to study, then looked slowly to the left. No Teresa. He turned a page in the book and stared at some math problems that scared him because he knew he would have to do them eventually. He looked at the right. Still no sign of her. He stretched out lazily in an attempt to disguise his snooping.

34　Then he saw her. She was sitting with a girlfriend under a plum tree. Victor moved to a table near her and daydreamed about taking her to a movie. When the bell sounded, Teresa looked up, and their eyes met. She smiled sweetly and gathered her books. Her next class was French, same as Victor's.

35　They were among the last students to arrive in class, so all the good desks in the back had already been taken. Victor was forced to sit near the front, a few desks away from Teresa, while Mr. Bueller wrote French words on the chalkboard. The bell rang, and Mr. Bueller wiped his hands, turned to the class, and said, "*Bonjour.*[4]"

36　"*Bonjour,*" braved a few students.

37　"*Bonjour,*" Victor whispered. He wondered if Teresa heard him.

38　Mr. Bueller said that if the students studied hard, at the end of the year they could go to France and be understood by the populace.

39　One kid raised his hand and asked, "What's 'populace'?"

40　"The people, the people of France."

41　Mr. Bueller asked if anyone knew French. Victor raised his hand, wanting to impress Teresa. The teacher beamed and said, "*Très bien. Parlez-vous français?*[5]"

42　Victor didn't know what to say. The teacher wet his lips and asked something else in French. The room grew silent. Victor felt all eyes staring at him. He tried to bluff his way out by making noises that sounded French.

43　"La me vave me con le grandma," he said uncertainly.

44　Mr. Bueller, wrinkling his face in curiosity, asked him to speak up.

45　Great rosebushes of red bloomed on Victor's cheeks. A river of nervous sweat ran down his palms. He felt awful. Teresa sat a few desks away, no doubt thinking he was a fool. Without looking at Mr. Bueller, Victor mumbled, 'Frenchie oh wewe gee in September."

46　Mr. Bueller asked Victor to repeat what he said.

47　"Frenchie oh wewe gee in September," Victor repeated.

48　Mr. Bueller understood that the boy didn't know French and turned away. He walked to the blackboard and pointed to the words on the board with his steel-edged ruler.

49　"*Le bateau,*" he sang.

50　"*Le bateau,*" the students repeated.

---

4. **bonjour** (French) hello
5. **Très bien. Parlez-vous français?** (French) Very good. Do you speak French?

NOTES

51 *"Le bateau est sur l'eau,"* he sang.

52 *"Le bateau est sur l'eau."*

53 Victor was too weak from failure to join the class. He stared at the board and wished he had taken Spanish, not French. Better yet, he wished he could start his life over. He had never been so embarrassed. He bit his thumb until he tore off a sliver of skin.

54 The bell sounded for fifth period, and Victor shot out of the room, avoiding the stares of the other kids, but had to return for his math book. He looked sheepishly at the teacher, who was erasing the board, then widened his eyes in terror at Teresa who stood in front of him. "I didn't know you knew French," she said. "That was good."

55 Mr. Bueller looked at Victor, and Victor looked back. Oh please, don't say anything, Victor pleaded with his eyes. I'll wash your car, mow your lawn, walk your dog—anything! I'll be your best student, and I'll clean your erasers after school.

56 Mr. Bueller shuffled through the papers on his desk. He smiled and hummed as he sat down to work. He remembered his college years when he dated a girlfriend in borrowed cars. She thought he was rich because each time he picked her up he had a different car. It was fun until he had spent all his money on her and had to write home to his parents because he was broke.

57 Victor couldn't stand to look at Teresa. He was sweaty with shame. "Yeah, well, I picked up a few things from movies and books and stuff like that." They left the class together. Teresa asked him if he would help her with her French.

58 "Sure, anytime," Victor said.

59 "I won't be bothering you, will I?"

60 "Oh no, I like being bothered."

61 *"Bonjour."* Teresa said, leaving him outside her next class. She smiled and pushed wisps of hair from her face.

62 "Yeah, right, *bonjour,*" Victor said. He turned and headed to his class. The rosebuds of shame on his face became bouquets of love. Teresa is a great girl, he thought. And Mr. Bueller is a good guy.

63 He raced to metal shop. After metal shop there was biology, and after biology a long sprint to the public library, where he checked out three French textbooks.

64 He was going to like seventh grade.

First Read

Read "Seventh Grade." After you read, complete the Think Questions below.

THINK QUESTIONS

1. What decision does Victor make on the first day of seventh grade, and why does he make it? Cite textual evidence from the selection to support your answer.

2. Why does Michael believe that "scowling" will impress his female classmates? How does Victor react to his friend's idea? Cite textual evidence in your response.

3. Why does Victor pretend that he already knows how to speak French? Does he succeed in achieving his goal? Why or why not? Cite textual evidence from the selection to support your answer.

4. Find the word **anxious** in paragraph 13 of "Seventh Grade." Use context clues in the surrounding sentences, as well as the sentence in which the word appears, to determine the word's meaning. Write your definition here, and identify clues that helped you figure out its meaning.

5. Use context clues to determine the meaning of **automatically** as it is used in paragraph 24 in "Seventh Grade." Write your definition here, and identify clues that helped you figure out the meaning. Then check the meaning in a dictionary.

Skill:
Setting

Use the Checklist to analyze Setting in "Seventh Grade." Refer to the sample student annotations about Setting in the text.

••• CHECKLIST FOR SETTING

In order to identify how particular elements of a story or drama interact, note the following:

- ✓ the setting of the story

- ✓ note the characters in the text and the problems they face

- ✓ how the events of the plot unfold, and how that affects the setting and characters

- ✓ how the setting shapes the characters and plot

To analyze how particular elements of a story or drama interact, consider the following questions as a guide:

- ✓ What is the setting(s) of the story?

- ✓ How does the setting affect the characters and plot?

- ✓ How does the setting contribute to or help solve the conflict?

- ✓ How do the characters' decisions affect the plot and setting(s)?

SETTING

sync•skills

Skill:
Setting

Reread paragraphs 13–19 of "Seventh Grade." Then, using the Checklist on the previous page, answer the multiple-choice questions below.

⟳ YOUR TURN

1. The description of Victor's homeroom in paragraph 13 suggests that —

   ○ A. the school year will be difficult for the students.
   ○ B. the school year will take a dangerous turn.
   ○ C. the school year will be similar to the previous year.
   ○ D. the school year will bring new opportunities for Victor.

2. How does the setting affect Victor's plan to have a conversation with Teresa in paragraph 17?

   ○ A. Their shared class gives Victor an idea of what to say to Teresa.
   ○ B. Like Teresa, Victor is interested in taking ballet.
   ○ C. Their teacher's presence makes Victor feel self-conscious.
   ○ D. Victor knows exactly what he wants to say to Teresa.

3. What does Victor's reaction to his conversation with Teresa, in paragraph 19, reveal about his character?

   ○ A. Victor should have scowled at Teresa instead of trying to talk to her.
   ○ B. Victor realizes he should have been more kind and honest with Teresa.
   ○ C. Victor should have waited until French class to talk to Teresa.
   ○ D. Victor thinks he will never be able to impress Teresa.

Skill:
Compare and Contrast

Use the Checklist to analyze Compare and Contrast in "Seventh Grade."

••• CHECKLIST FOR COMPARE AND CONTRAST

In order to compare and contrast texts within and across different forms and genres, do the following:

✓ first, choose two or more texts with similar subjects or topic

✓ next, identify the qualities or characteristics of each form or genre

✓ then highlight and annotate each text looking for

• ways in which the texts are similar and different

• how each author approaches the topic or subject

• the words and actions of characters or individuals or important events

• textual evidence that reveals each text's theme or central message

To compare and contrast texts within and across different forms or genres, consider the following questions:

✓ In what ways do the texts I have chosen have similar subjects or topics?

✓ What are the qualities or characteristics of each form or genre?

✓ How are the texts similar and different?

✓ How does each author approach the topic or subject?

✓ Have I looked at the words and actions of characters or individuals? What are the important events that occur in each text?

✓ What is the theme or central message of each text?

Skill:
Compare and Contrast

Reread paragraphs 7 and 8 and 11 and 12 of "Seventh Grade" and paragraphs 4 and 5 and 7–9 of *Stargirl*. Then, using the Checklist on the previous page, complete the chart below to compare and contrast the passages.

⟳ YOUR TURN

	Observation Options
A	Victor copies Michael's scowling to see if it can make him appear more handsome.
B	Stargirl sings "Happy Birthday" to Alan Ferko in the cafeteria.
C	Michael scowls to make himself look handsome.
D	Kevin says Stargirl's strange behavior will cause problems for her in school.
E	Other characters notice and have reactions to the unusual behavior.
F	Characters demonstrate unusual behavior.

"Seventh Grade"	Both	*Stargirl*

Close Read

Reread "Seventh Grade." As you reread, complete the Skills Focus questions below. Then use your answers and annotations from the questions to help you complete the Write activity.

◎ SKILLS FOCUS

1. Identify details that show how Victor reveals himself during English class. Explain why you think he is not behaving in a more cautious and guarded manner.

2. Identify evidence that describes how Victor feels during French class. How do his peers and the setting affect him?

3. What lesson is learned in this text about being a young person in school?

4. Both *Stargirl* and "Seventh Grade" deal with potentially embarrassing situations in a school setting. Identify one of those situations in "Seventh Grade." Explain the cause and the outcome of the situation. Then describe how it compares and contrasts with the content in *Stargirl*.

5. Identify textual evidence that shows how Victor is able to avoid a conflict with Mr. Bueller in front of Teresa. Describe how Mr. Bueller is similar to Victor.

✏ WRITE

COMPARE AND CONTRAST: *Stargirl* takes place in high school, while "Seventh Grade" is set in middle school. Write a short response in which you choose two characters, one from each work of fiction, and compare and contrast how the school setting creates conflict for the characters. Use evidence from each text to support your analysis.

The Monsters Are Due on Maple Street

DRAMA
Rod Serling
1960

Introduction

Rod Serling (1924–1975), creator of the science fiction television series *The Twilight Zone,* was one of the most popular writers in television history. One of his best-known scripts, "The Monsters Are Due on Maple Street" is about the reaction of a group of neighbors to a mysterious shadow that passes over their suburban street. After homes lose power and car batteries go dead, a neighborhood boy suggests that alien invaders in human form are responsible for the strange events. As power flickers back on here and there, neighbors become increasingly alarmed, turning their suspicions against one another.

"... maybe one family isn't what we think they are."

Copyright © BookheadEd Learning, LLC

NOTES

⚙ **Skill:**
Plot

This event must be the inciting incident. Goodman's car is the only one in the neighborhood that works, which causes a crowd to approach him. Goodman is upset and starts to defend himself. The power outage has turned this typical town into a tense mob.

Steve seems to be joking about monsters, but then things get serious. He suggests that Goodman and his family are different or hiding something. It seems like more conflict is about to start!

from Act I

1   GOODMAN. Wait a minute now. You keep your distance—all of you. So I've got a car that starts by itself—well, that's a freak thing, I admit it. But does that make me some kind of a criminal or something? I don't know why the car works—it just does!

2   [*This stops the crowd momentarily and now* GOODMAN, *still backing away, goes toward his front porch. He goes up the steps and then stops to stand facing the mob.*

3   *We see a long shot of* STEVE *as he comes through the crowd.*]

4   STEVE. [*Quietly.*] We're all on a monster kick, Les. Seems that the general impression holds that maybe one family isn't what we think they are. Monsters from outer space or something. Different than us. Fifth columnists[1] from the vast beyond. [*He chuckles.*] You know anybody that might fit that description around here on Maple Street?

5   GOODMAN. What is this, a gag or something? This a practical joke or something?

6   [*We see a close-up of the porch light as it suddenly goes out. There's a murmur from the group.*]

7   GOODMAN. Now I suppose that's supposed to incriminate me! The light goes on and off. That really does it, doesn't it? [*He look around the faces of the people.*] I just don't understand this— [*He wets his lips, looking from face to face.*] Look, you all know me. We've lived here five years. Right in this house. We're no different from any of the rest of you! We're no different at all. Really . . . this whole thing is just . . . just weird—

---

1. **Fifth columnists** a term commonly used in the 20th century for any secretive group of operators attempting to undermine a larger group from within

---

8 WOMAN. Well, if that's the case, Les Goodman, explain why— [*She stops suddenly, clamping her mouth shut.*]

9 GOODMAN. [*Softly.*] Explain what?

10 STEVE. [*Interjecting*] Look, let's forget this—

11 CHARLIE. [*Overlapping him.*] Go ahead, let her talk. What about it? Explain what?

12 WOMAN. [*A little **reluctantly**.*] Well . . . sometimes I go to bed late at night. A couple of times . . . a couple of times I'd come out on the porch and I'd see Mr. Goodman here in the wee hours of the morning standing out in front of his house . . . looking up at the sky. [*She looks around the circle of faces.*] That's right, looking up at the sky as if . . . as if he were waiting for something. [*A pause.*] As if he were looking for something.

13 [*There's a murmur of reaction from the crowd again.*

14 *We cut suddenly to a group shot. As* GOODMAN *starts toward them, they back away frightened.*]

15 GOODMAN. You know really . . . this is for laughs. You know what I'm guilty of? [*He laughs.*] I'm guilty of **insomnia.** Now what's the penalty for insomnia? [*At this point the laugh, the humor, leaves his voice.*] Did you hear what I said? I said it was insomnia. [*A pause as he looks around, then shouts.*] I said it was insomnia! You fools. You scared, frightened rabbits, you. You're sick people, do you know that? You're sick people—all of you! And you don't even know what you're starting because let me tell you . . . let me tell you—this thing you're starting—that should frighten you. As God is my witness . . . you're letting something begin here that's a nightmare!

from Act II

16 CHARLIE'S VOICE. [*Shrill, from across the street.*] You best watch who you're seen with, Steve! Until we get this all straightened out, you ain't exactly above suspicion yourself.

17 STEVE. [*Whirling around toward him.*] Or you, Charlie. Or any of us, it seems. From age eight on up.

18 WOMAN. What I'd like to know is—what are we gonna do? Just stand around here all night?

Skill: Dramatic Elements and Structure

Steve is yelling at the other characters. The conflict is getting worse and the suspense is building.

There's a lot of quick back-and-forth dialogue here. It feels hostile. I think this whole story is about to end in tragedy.

Skill: Plot

Steve is getting frustrated and suggests getting rid of suspects with a firing squad! Then, Don accuses Steve of doing things in his basement. The neighbors are turning on one another because they are scared. This story is moving so quickly!

19 CHARLIE. There's nothin' else we can do! [*He turns back looking toward* STEVE *and* GOODMAN *again.*] One of 'em'll tip their hand[2]. They got to.

20 STEVE [*Raising his voice.*] There's something you can do, Charlie. You could go home and keep your mouth shut. You could quit strutting around like a self-appointed hanging judge and just climb into bed and forget it.

21 CHARLIE. You sound real **anxious** to have that happen, Steve. I think we better keep our eye on you too!

22 DON. [*As if he were taking the bit in his teeth, takes a hesitant step to the front.*] I think everything might as well come out now. [*He turns toward* STEVE.] Your wife's done plenty of talking, Steve, about how odd you are!

23 CHARLIE. [*Picking this up, his eyes widening.*] Go ahead, tell us what she's said. [*We see a long shot of* STEVE *as he walks toward them from across the street.*]

24 STEVE. Go ahead, what's my wife said? Let's get it all out. Let's pick out every **idiosyncrasy** of every man, woman, and child on the street. And then we might as well set up some kind of kangaroo court[3]. How about a firing squad[4] at dawn, Charlie, so we can get rid of all the suspects? Narrow them down. Make it easier for you.

25 DON. There's no need gettin' so upset, Steve. It's just that . . . well . . . Myra's talked about how there's been plenty of nights you spent hours down in your basement workin' on some kind of radio or something. Well, none of us have ever seen that radio—

26 [*By this time* STEVE *has reached the group. He stands there defiantly close to them.*]

27 CHARLIE. Go ahead, Steve. What kind of "radio set" you workin' on? I never seen it. Neither has anyone else. Who you talk to on that radio set? And who talks to you?

28 STEVE. I'm surprised at you, Charlie. How come you're so **dense** all of a sudden? [*A pause.*] Who do I talk to? I talk to monsters from outer space. I talk to three-headed green men who fly over here in what look like meteors.

29 [STEVE'S *wife steps down from the porch, bites her lip, calls out.*]

---

2. **tip their hand** an expression in cards or poker for unintentionally revealing one's secrets or intentions
3. **kangaroo court** a term for an unofficial or mob-like court that operates outside of basic judicial principles
4. **firing squad** a method of execution in which a person is shot repeatedly from close range

30   MRS. BRAND. Steve! Steve, please. [*Then looking around, frightened, she walks toward the group.*] It's just a ham radio⁵ set, that's all. I bought him a book on it myself. It's just a ham radio set. A lot of people have them. I can show it to you. It's right down in the basement.

31   STEVE. [*whirls around toward her*] Show them nothing! If they want to look inside our house—let them get a search warrant.

32   CHARLIE. Look, buddy. You can't afford to—

33   STEVE. [*Interrupting*] Charlie, don't tell me what I can afford! And stop telling me who's dangerous and who isn't and who's safe and who's a menace. [*He turns to the group and shouts.*] And you're with him, too—all of you! You're standing here all set to crucify—all set to find a scapegoat—all desperate to point some kind of finger at a neighbor! Well now look, friends, the only thing that's gonna happen is that we'll eat each other up alive—

34   [*He stops abruptly as CHARLIE suddenly grabs his arm.*]

35   CHARLIE. [*In a hushed voice*] That's not the only thing that can happen to us.

36   [*Cut to a long shot looking down the street. A figure has suddenly materialized in the gloom and in the silence we can hear the clickety-clack of slow, measured footsteps on concrete as the figure walks slowly toward them. One of the women lets out a stifled cry. The young mother grabs her boy as do a couple of others.*]

37   TOMMY. [*Shouting, frightened.*] It's the monster! It's the monster!

38   [*Another woman lets out a wail and the people fall back in a group, staring toward the darkness and the approaching figure.*

39   *We see a medium group shot of the people as they stand in the shadows watching. DON MARTIN joins them, carrying a shotgun. He holds it up.*]

40   DON. We may need this.

41   STEVE. A shotgun? [*He pulls it out of DON'S hand.*] Good Lord—will anybody think a thought around here? Will you people wise up? What good would a shotgun do against—

42   [*Now CHARLIE pulls the gun from STEVE's hand.*]

43   CHARLIE. No more talk, Steve. You're going to talk us into a grave! You'd let whatever's out there walk right over us, wouldn't yuh? Well, some of us won't!

---

5. **ham radio set** an amateur radio setup typically used for broadcasting or receiving messages

44 [*He swings the gun around to point it toward the sidewalk. The dark figure continues to walk toward them.*

45 *The group stands there, fearful,* **apprehensive**, *mothers clutching children, men standing in front of wives.* CHARLIE *slowly raises the gun. As the figure gets closer and closer he suddenly pulls the trigger. The sound of it explodes in the stillness. There is a long angle shot looking down the figure, who suddenly lets out a small cry, stumbles forward onto his knees and then falls forward on his face.* DON, CHARLIE, *and* STEVE *race forward over to him.* STEVE *is there first and turns the man over. Now the crowd gathers around them.*]

46 STEVE [Slowly looks up] It's Pete Van Horn.

47 DON. [*In a hushed voice.*] Pete Van Horn! He was just gonna go over to the next block to see if the power was on—

48 WOMAN. You killed him, Charlie. You shot him dead!

49 CHARLIE. [*Looks around the circle of faces, his eyes frightened, his face contorted.*] But . . . but I didn't know who he was. I certainly didn't know who he was. He comes walkin' out of the darkness—how am I supposed to know who he was? [*He grabs* STEVE.] Steve—you know why I shot! How was I supposed to know he wasn't a monster or something? [*He grabs* DON *now.*] We're all scared of the same thing, I was just tryin' to . . . trying' to protect my home, that's all! Look, all of you, that's all I was tryin' to do. [*He looks down wildly at the body.*] I didn't know it was somebody we knew! I didn't know—

50 [*There's a sudden hush and then an intake of breath. We see a medium shot of the living room window of* CHARLIE'S *house. The window is not lit, but suddenly the house lights come on behind it.*]

51 WOMAN. [*In a very hushed voice.*] Charlie. . . Charlie. . . the lights just went on in your house. Why did the lights just go on?

52 DON. What about it, Charlie? How come you're the only one with lights now?

53 GOODMAN. That's what I'd like to know.

©1960 by Rod Serling, The Monsters Are Due on Maple Street. Reproduced by permission of Carolyn Serling.

First Read

Read "The Monsters Are Due on Maple Street." After you read, complete the Think Questions below.

☁ THINK QUESTIONS

1. Why are the Maple Street neighbors suspicious of Les Goodman? Respond with direct evidence or inferences from the text.

2. Why are the Maple Street neighbors suspicious of Steve? Include evidence from the text to support your response.

3. Why does Tommy shout, "It's the monster! It's the monster!"? Support your answer with textual evidence.

4. Use context clues to determine the meaning of **insomnia** as it is used in paragraph 15 of "The Monsters Are Due on Maple Street." Write your definition here and identify clues that helped you figure out the meaning. Then check the meaning in a dictionary.

5. Find the word **dense** in paragraph 28 of "The Monsters Are Due on Maple Street." Use context clues in the surrounding sentences, as well as the sentence in which the word appears, to determine the word's meaning. Write your definition here and identify clues that helped you figure out the meaning.

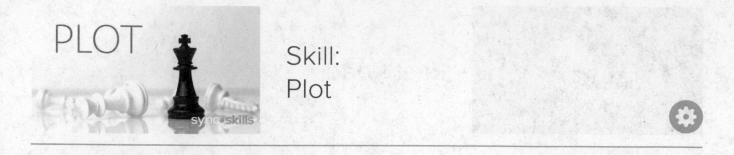

PLOT

Skill:
Plot

Use the Checklist to analyze Plot in "The Monsters Are Due on Maple Street." Refer to the sample student annotations about Plot in the text.

••• CHECKLIST FOR PLOT

In order to identify particular elements of a story or drama, note the following:

- ✓ setting details

- ✓ character details, including their thoughts, actions, and descriptions

- ✓ notable incidents or events in the plot

- ✓ characters or setting details that may have caused an event to occur

- ✓ the central conflict and the characters who are involved

- ✓ dialogue between or among characters

- ✓ instances when setting interferes with a character's motivations

To analyze how particular elements of a story or drama interact, consider the following questions:

- ✓ How do the events of the plot unfold in the story?

- ✓ How do characters respond or change as the plot advances?

- ✓ How does the setting shape the characters or the plot?

- ✓ How does a particular scene in the story contribute to the development of the plot?

PLOT

sync skills

Skill:
Plot

⚙

Reread paragraphs 6–15 of "The Monsters Are Due on Maple Street." Then, using the Checklist on the previous page, answer the multiple-choice questions below.

🔁 YOUR TURN

1. This question has two parts. First, answer Part A. Then, answer Part B.

   Part A: What effect do the woman's words and actions in paragraph 12 have on the plot and conflict?

   ○ A. The woman's words and actions cause Steve to interject.
   ○ B. The woman's words and actions cause the crowd to laugh at Goodman.
   ○ C. The woman's words and actions cause confusion.
   ○ D. The woman's words and actions cause the crowd to fear Goodman.

   Part B: Which piece of evidence best supports your answer to Part A?

   ○ A. *"We cut suddenly to a group shot. As* GOODMAN *starts toward them, they back away frightened."*
   ○ B. "You know really . . . this is for laughs. You know what I'm guilty of? [*He laughs.*]"
   ○ C. "STEVE. [*Interjecting*] Look, let's forget this—"
   ○ D. "[*A little reluctantly.*] Well . . . sometimes I go to bed late at night."

2. How does Goodman's reaction in paragraph 7 advance the conflict of the story?

   ○ A. Goodman feels misunderstood. His body language reflects sadness, which creates tension.
   ○ B. Goodman is upset. His body language reflects fear and anxiousness, which creates tension.
   ○ C. Goodman is telling the crowd that he is not to blame. He does not understand their accusations, which creates tension.
   ○ D. Goodman is laughing and looking at the crowd. His body language reflects fear, which creates tension.

Skill: Dramatic Elements and Structure

Use the Checklist to analyze Dramatic Elements and Structure in "The Monsters Are Due on Maple Street." Refer to the sample student annotations about Dramatic Elements and Structure in the text.

••• CHECKLIST FOR DRAMATIC ELEMENTS AND STRUCTURE

In order to identify the dramatic elements and structure of a drama, note the following:

✓ the form of the drama, such as

  • comedy, or a drama that has a happy ending

  • tragedy, or a drama that ends in death or sadness

✓ how the drama's structure, including its acts and scenes, advances the plot

✓ the setting of the play and how it affects the characters and plot

✓ the language of the play as spoken by characters

✓ the information in stage directions, including lighting, sound, and set, as well as details about characters, including exits and entrances

To analyze how a drama's form or structure contributes to its meaning, consider the following questions:

✓ How does the use of dialogue and stage directions reveal aspects of the characters and contribute to the drama's meaning?

✓ How is each act or scene structured? How do characters enter and leave, how do they speak to each other, and what happens as a result?

✓ How do specific acts or scenes develop the plot or advance the conflict?

✓ How does the drama's form contribute to the theme or message?

Skill: Dramatic Elements and Structure

Reread paragraphs 48–53 of "The Monsters Are Due on Maple Street." Then, using the Checklist on the previous page, answer the multiple-choice questions below.

YOUR TURN

1. This question has two parts. First, answer Part A. Then, answer Part B.

   Part A: What does Charlie's dialogue in paragraph 49 suggest about the drama's deeper message or meaning?

   ○ A. It explains why Charlie shot Pete Van Horn.

   ○ B. It suggests a message about the importance of protecting family.

   ○ C. It suggests a message about how people fear the unknown.

   ○ D. It suggests that Charlie is an evil character.

   Part B: Select evidence from paragraph 49 that best supports your answer in Part A.

   ○ A. "How was I supposed to know he wasn't a monster or something? [*He grabs* DON *now.*] We're all scared of the same thing . . ."

   ○ B. "I was just tryin' to . . . trying to protect my home, that's all!"

   ○ C. "[*Looks around the circle of faces, his eyes frightened, his face contorted.*]"

   ○ D. "[*He looks down wildly at the body.*] I didn't know it was somebody we knew! I didn't know—"

2. The stage directions in paragraph 49 show that Charlie feels —

   ○ A. confusion

   ○ B. panic

   ○ C. regret

   ○ D. anger

Close Read

Reread "The Monsters Are Due on Maple Street." As you reread, complete the Skills Focus questions below. Then use your answers and annotations from the questions to help you complete the Write activity.

◎ SKILLS FOCUS

1. The character Charlie is the most accusatory and paranoid of the neighbors. Identify dialogue and/or stage directions that show this, and explain how his qualities affect the other people in the neighborhood or events in the plot.

2. Steve is portrayed as a more rational character than the other neighbors. Identify dialogue and/or stage directions that support Steve's characterization as a level-headed person, and explain why this makes him the "hero" of the story.

3. Identify textual evidence that shows how the characters scapegoat or blame each other. What does this evidence reveal about the main conflict of the drama?

4. Identify and highlight the turning point and unfortunate resolution. Explain how those events contribute to the overall meaning or theme of the play.

5. Explain what message is suggested about society and conflict. Cite textual evidence to support your response.

✏ WRITE

LITERARY ANALYSIS: How does Rod Serling use plot and dramatic elements and structure to convey a message about conflict in society? Write a short response in which you answer this question. Specify one message, and explain how plot and dramatic elements and structure help to convey it. Use textual evidence to support your answer.

The Skin I'm In

FICTION
Sharon G. Flake
1998

Introduction

American young adult literature author Sharon G. Flake (b. 1955) tells evocative stories that dig deep into the intersection between race and gender in late 20th- and early 21st-century America. Her first and most widely-known novel, *The Skin I'm In*, tells the story of 13-year old Maleeka Madison, who is mired in all of the trials and tribulations of teenage self-discovery. On top of this, Maleeka faces yet another challenge—finding self-love and self-acceptance in her dark skin and African features in a world that seems to devalue both.

"Everybody starts talking at once, asking her questions. Miss Saunders answers 'em all."

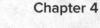

Skill:
Point of View

The narrator uses the pronoun "I," so Maleeka must be the narrator and is telling the story. She's only revealing her thoughts. It must be a limited point of view.

It seems as if Maleeka's face says something funny or bad to the world, because she laughs when she reads the prompt. Maybe Maleeka doesn't like the way she looks.

Chapter 4

1 When the second bell rings, I run to Miss Saunders's class like somebody set my shoes on fire. It don't help none. Soon as I walk in, I know I'm in trouble. Everybody's got their head down and they're writing. Miss Saunders nods for me to take out paper and get to my seat. "What does your face say to the world?" is written on the blackboard. I laugh, only it comes out like a sneeze through my nose.

2 Miss Saunders is collecting papers before I even got three sentences down on my paper. She knows I just slipped in. That don't stop her from asking me to answer the question, though.

3 "My face?" I point to myself.

4 "Maleeka's face says she needs to stay out of the sun," Larry Baker says, covering his face with a book.

5 "Naw, man," Gregory Williams says. "Maleeka's face says, Black is beautiful."

6 Miss Saunders don't say nothing. She just crosses her arms and gets real quiet. She don't care if she done embarrassed me again.

7 "Maleeka?" she says.

8 I don't answer her question or look her way. I eye the ceiling and count the blobs of gum hanging there like pretty-colored snot.

9 "Can anybody else tell me what their face says to the world?" Miss Saunders asks. Her gold bangles[1] jingle while she makes her way around the room. Miss Saunders is as quiet as a tiger sneaking up on its **supper.** It's them Italian leather shoes of hers, I guess.

10 Malcolm Moore raises his hand. Malcolm is fine. He's got long, straight hair. Skin the color of a butterscotch milkshake. Gray, sad eyes. He's half and

---

1. **bangles** bracelets or anklets worn as accessories

half—got a white dad and a black momma. He's lucky. He looks more like his dad than his mom.

11 "My face says I'm all that," Malcolm says, rubbing them six chin hairs he calls a beard. "It says to the homies, I'm the doctor of love. I'm good to ya and good for ya."

12 Everybody laughs. Faith, his girlfriend of the week, throws a pencil across the room. It bounces off the back of his chair, and lands between his big feet. Miss Saunders gives Faith the eye, letting her know to cut it out.

13 When the laughing's done, hands go up. Some folks say funny stuff about their face. Others is real serious. Like John-John. He says his face tells the world he doesn't take no stuff. That people better respect him, or else. I never seen nothing like that in John-John's face. He looks more scared than mean. I guess there ain't no **accounting** for what folks see in their own mirrors.

14 When Miss Saunders asks, "What's my face say?" don't nobody say nothing.

15 "Don't get all closed-mouthed, now," she says. "I hear you whispering in the hall. Laughing at me." She walks the aisles again. She stops by me and sits on my desk. "Faces say more than you think. Even mine. Don't be shy. Say what's on your mind."

16 My hand goes up. I figure she's embarrassed me twice since she's been here this week. Now it's her turn. "Not to hurt your feelings...but...I think it says, you know, you're a freak."

17 "That's cold," Chrystal Johnson says, frowning.

18 Miss Saunders put her hands up to her chin like she's praying. She gets up and walks the room, pacing. We don't say nothing. We just listen to the clock tick. **Shuffle** our papers. Watch for some reaction from Miss Saunders.

19 "Freak," she says. "I saw that too when I was young." Then she explains how she was born with her face like that. How when she was little her parents had the preacher pray over it, the old folks work their roots on it, and her grandmother use some **concoction** to change the color of that **blotch** on her cheek so it matched the rest of her skin. Miss Saunders says none of the stuff she tried on her face worked. So she finally figured she'd better love what God gave her.

20 "Liking myself didn't come overnight," she says, "I took a lot of wrong turns to find out who I really was. You will, too." Everybody starts talking at once, asking her questions. Miss Saunders answers 'em all. Some kids even go up to her face and stare and point. She lets them do it too, like she's proud of her face or something.

Skill:
Point of View

Miss Saunders's actions and dialogue show that she has a lot of self-confidence! I can tell from Maleeka's thoughts that she still has a contrasting view. Maleeka seems surprised that the teacher is proud of her appearance.

NOTES

21 Then Miss Saunders comes over to my desk and stares down at me. "It takes a long time to accept yourself for who you are. To see the poetry in your walk," she says, shaking her hips like she's doing some African dance. Kids bust out laughing. "To look in the mirror and like what you see, even when it doesn't look like anybody else's idea of beauty."

Excerpted from *The Skin I'm In* by Sharon G. Flake, published by Hyperion Books.

THE SKIN I'M IN

First Read

Read *The Skin I'm In*. After you read, complete the Think Questions below.

☁ THINK QUESTIONS

1. What is it about Maleeka's appearance that makes Larry Baker say she needs to stay out of the sun? Why is this significant to the conversation Miss Saunders is having with the class?

2. What does John-John say his face says to the world? Why doesn't Maleeka believe him?

3. What is it about Miss Saunders's appearance that the students primarily make fun of? Explain why you believe they make fun of it.

4. Read the following dictionary definition:

   account
   ac•count /əˈkount/

   noun

   1. a detailed record of money paid and received
   2. a particular description or report of something that happened

   verb

   1. to form or make up a part of something
   2. to offer a reason or explanation for something

   Which definition most closely matches the meaning of **accounting** as it is used in paragraph 13? Write the correct definition of *accounting* here and explain how you figured out the correct meaning.

5. Miss Saunders says that her grandmother tried to use a **concoction** on her face. Based on context clues, what do you think the word *concoction* means? Write your best definition of *concoction* here and explain how you figured it out.

Skill:
Point of View

Use the Checklist to analyze Point of View in *The Skin I'm In*. Refer to the sample student annotations about Point of View in the text.

••• CHECKLIST FOR POINT OF VIEW

In order to identify different points of view, note the following:

✓ the speaker(s) or narrator(s)

✓ how much the narrator(s) or speaker(s) knows and reveals

✓ how the author develops different points of view, through dialogue or story events

✓ what the narrator(s) or speaker(s) says or does that reveals how they feel about other characters and events

✓ how the point of view of the narrator(s) or speaker(s) contrasts with the points of view of other characters in the narrative

To analyze how an author develops and contrasts different points of view of different characters or narrators in a text, consider the following questions:

✓ Is the narrator or speaker objective, or does he or she mislead the reader? How?

✓ What is the narrator's or the speaker's point of view?

  • Is the narrator or speaker "all-knowing," or omniscient?

  • Is the narrator or speaker limited to revealing the thoughts and feelings of one character?

  • Are there multiple narrators or speakers telling the story?

✓ How does the narrator or speaker reveal his or her thoughts about the events or the other characters in the story or poem? How do the narrator's experiences or cultural background affect his or her thoughts?

✓ How does the author reveal different points of view in the story?

✓ How do these different points of view compare and contrast with one another?

Skill:
Point of View

Reread paragraphs 16–19 of *The Skin I'm In*. Then, using the Checklist on the previous page, answer the multiple-choice questions below.

⟳ YOUR TURN

1. This question has two parts. First, answer Part A. Then, answer Part B.

   Part A: What is Miss Saunders's point of view about loving her appearance?

   ○ A. Miss Saunders used to hate her appearance, but she learned to love it.
   ○ B. Miss Saunders used to love her appearance, but now she hates it.
   ○ C. Miss Saunders hates her appearance because people call her a freak.
   ○ D. Miss Saunders has always loved her appearance and has never tried to change it.

   Part B: Which line from the passage supports your answer in Part A?

   ○ A. I figure she's embarrassed me twice since she's been here this week. Now it's her turn.
   ○ B. Miss Saunders put her hands up to her chin like she's praying.
   ○ C. Then she explains how she was born with her face like that.
   ○ D. So she finally figured she'd better love what God gave her.

2. Which sentence from the story lets you know this is limited point of view?

   ○ A. Then she explains how she was born with her face like that.
   ○ B. "I saw that too when I was young."
   ○ C. My hand goes up. I figure she's embarrassed me twice since she's been here this week.
   ○ D. "That's cold," Chrystal Johnson says, frowning.

Close Read

THE SKIN I'M IN

Reread *The Skin I'm In*. As you reread, complete the Skills Focus questions below. Then use your answers and annotations from the questions to help you complete the Write activity.

◎ SKILLS FOCUS

1. How do the first few paragraphs indicate that the narrator is using a limited point of view? Highlight evidence from the text, and make annotations to support your explanation.

2. Identify dialogue and actions that reveal Maleeka's classmates' views on self-love and their own appearances.

3. Identify dialogue and actions that reveal Miss Saunders's point of view on self-acceptance and self-love. Explain why this point of view might be surprising to some of her students.

4. Identify evidence of how Miss Saunders's point of view about her appearance changed over time and what led to that change. What lesson or theme is suggested by Miss Saunders's change?

5. What does Maleeka do, say, or think to reveal her point of view on self-acceptance and self-love? How is Maleeka's point of view in conflict with her classmates' or her teacher's points of view?

✎ WRITE

LITERARY ANALYSIS: In this excerpt of *The Skin I'm In*, Maleeka confronts how she feels about herself while learning about others' views on self-love and self-acceptance. How is Maleeka's point of view different from those of the other students and Miss Saunders? How does the author reveal and contrast these views? Use textual evidence, including character dialogue, actions, and thoughts, to support your response.

Mad

POETRY
Naomi Shihab Nye
2000

Introduction

The author of numerous books and collections of poetry, contemporary Arab American poet Naomi Shihab Nye (b. 1952) explores the landscape of the human spirit through allegory, transformative imagery, and the lens of her unique cultural perspective. In this poem, "Mad," Nye sheds new light on the emotional bonds between mothers and their children.

"It gets cold at night on the moon."

1   I got mad at my mother

2   so I flew to the moon.

3   I could still see our house

4   so little in the distance

5   with its **pointed** roof.

6   My mother stood in the front yard

7   like a pin dot

8   searching for me.

9   She **looked** left and right for me.

10   She looked deep and far.

11   Then I whistled and she **tipped** her head.

12   It gets cold at night on the moon.

13   My mother sent up a silver **thread**

14   for me to slide down on.

15   She knows me so well.

16   She knows I like silver.

✏ WRITE

PERSONAL RESPONSE: This poem is about making up with a loved one after getting angry. Write about a time you made up with a family member or friend after a disagreement or fight. What in the poem reminds you of your disagreement or fight? Was anything different? Support your response with evidence from the text.

In the Year 1974

INFORMATIONAL TEXT
Oscar Casares
2005

Introduction

Critically acclaimed author Oscar Casares (b. 1964) is a Texas native who teaches creative writing at the University of Texas at Austin. "In the Year 1974" recalls the summer when ten-year-old Oscar "discovered the world," as he describes it in hindsight. With his aging parents firmly set in their ways, young Oscar is sheltered from the world until he takes a trip to visit his older sister in Austin, where he finds an entirely unfamiliar and exciting world. Upon returning home to Brownsville, he's eager to share a thrilling culinary discovery with his parents—the pepperoni pizza.

"It was as though I'd crossed into another world, one my parents never knew existed."

1   It was only a few months after I turned ten that I discovered the world. Before this time, I had spent most of my life in Brownsville, at the southernmost point of not only Texas but also the continental United States. One of our few excursions from home was driving across the international bridge to Matamoros[1] so I could get what my father considered a "decent" haircut, by which he meant a very short haircut that cost less than a dollar, tip included. The barber would bring out a special cushioned board and lay it across the armrests of the chair. Then I'd climb up and sit still for my haircut, waiting patiently during those times when the barber had to stop and make a *ss-ss-ss* sound at a pretty girl passing in front of his shop. Afterward, my father and I would walk to Plaza Hidalgo, where he could get his boots shined and I could buy a candy from the man standing on the corner with the big glass case. I always went for the calabaza candies, which were made of a rich pumpkin and looked like jewels extracted from deep within the earth.

2   As far south as we were, I knew there was a world beyond Brownsville because my sister and two brothers had left town years earlier. When we drove to Houston to visit my brothers, one of them would take my mother to the mall so she could shop at the big department stores we didn't have at Amigoland Mall. After shopping, we'd go back to my brother's house, eat, rest, maybe eat again, maybe watch TV, and then go to sleep. A couple of days later, we'd get in the car and drive back to Brownsville. My parents weren't interested in seeing Houston. Houston was a big city with a lot of freeways where they were bound to get lost, and did, every time we visited, which was how I ended up seeing more of the city. My parents traveled to Houston to visit family, not to be running around getting lost. They had no interest in the roller coasters at Astroworld or ice-skating at the Galleria or anything else. My father worked as a livestock inspector for the USDA and spent a good part of his day patrolling the Rio Grande on horseback to make sure horses or cattle weren't being crossed into the country. During his rides he had been startled by rattlesnakes, bucked off his horse, and shot at by drug smugglers—he didn't need any more excitement in his life. Besides, it was usually hot in

---

1. **Matamoros** a Mexican city located right at the U.S. border, in the northeastern state of Tamaulipas

NOTES

Houston, and he hadn't worked out in the sun the other 51 weeks out of the year so he could drive to another city to sweat on his vacation.

3 I should mention that my parents were older than most parents with a ten-year-old in the house. My mother was 52 and my father was 60. Being older, they had developed certain habits that they weren't going to change. For instance, my father believed in sticking to certain meals. Food fell into three distinct **categories:** Mexican food, which he could eat every day and die a happy man; American food—meals like hamburgers, hot dogs, and fried chicken—which we ate occasionally; and other people's food, which included all the food he refused to eat. Whenever I suggested trying something different, like Chinese food, he'd look at me as if he and my mother might have brought the wrong baby home from the hospital.

4 As I understood it, this was my father's unstated **philosophy:** *We have our food—fajitas, tamales, tacos, enchiladas. It took our people many years to develop these foods. We even have two kinds of tortillas, flour and corn. So tell me why you want to eat other people's food? Leave their food alone. The* chinos *have their own food. They like that white rice. But do you see them eating our rice with those little sticks? No. The Germans, I don't know what they eat, but whatever it is, that's their business. The Italians, they like to add a lot of spices. I tried it one time and it gave me* agruras[2], *and then there I was, burping all night. Your mother had to make me an Alka-Seltzer. And you want me to eat other people's food?*

5 All of which meant that if my father ate carne con papas, I ate carne con papas. If he ate picadillo, I ate picadillo. If he ate taquitos, I ate taquitos. And so on, until 1974, the summer my sister, Sylvia, invited me to stay with her in Austin for two weeks. She and my brother-in-law were in their early twenties, and my nephew was only a year old. One of the first things we did in Austin was walk around the University of Texas, where my sister was a student. Then we rode the elevator all the way up to the top of the UT Tower, and I felt my ears pop for the first time. From the observation deck, I saw tiny people walking around on the street, but I couldn't tell which were the hippies and which were the ones with short hair. Some of my sister's friends wore their hair long, like the hippies I'd seen around town. Rolando had a handlebar mustache and hair down to his shoulders. He was the funniest of my sister's friends, and the smartest. You could ask him any math question, and he'd answer it as though he had a calculator stuck in his head. "What's fifty-six times seventeen?" I'd ask him. And he'd go, "Nine hundred fifty-two." That fast. Rolando came along the night we played putt-putt. He beat all of us because he knew how to hit his ball so it would go under the windmill just right. When we finished playing, he asked me if I wanted a **souvenir.** I said yes, thinking he was going

---

2. **agruras** (Spanish) heartburn

NOTES

to buy me a T-shirt at the front booth. But instead, he took my putter and tossed it over the fence, into some hedges. Then we all walked out, and Rolando grabbed the putter for me. "There's your souvenir," he said.

6   My last night in town, my sister and brother-in-law asked if I wanted pizza. "Pizza?" I said. I'd never actually tried the food. We drove to a Pizza Inn, and my brother-in-law ordered a pepperoni pizza. The waitress brought plates for everyone, even my baby nephew. I thought of my parents back home and what they might be eating that night. A few minutes later the waitress brought out a steaming pizza and placed it in front of us. None of it seemed real: the triangle shape of my slice, the perfectly round pepperonis, the doughy end crust, the gooey melted cheese. It was as though I'd crossed into another world, one my parents never knew existed. I was still several years away from leaving Brownsville, but in that moment I felt as far from home as I ever would.

7   My mother called the apartment that night.

8   "Guess what we ate?" I said.

9   "What?"

10   "Pizza!"

11   "Pizza?"

12   "Yeah, and when I get home, we're all going to get some."

13   "If that's really what you want, maybe we can try it." She sounded distracted. "Don't hang up," she said. "Somebody wants to talk to you."

14   "Are you having fun?" my father asked.

15   "Yes, sir."

16   "And you been behaving?"

17   "Yes, sir."

18   "That's a good boy." I could hear his stubble brushing against the receiver. "You need to be careful tomorrow, okay?"

19   "I will."

20   "We miss you, *mi'jo.*" He said it softly but clearly.

21   I hesitated for a second. "Okay, see you tomorrow."

22   The next morning my sister made me sit behind the bus driver. She said I wasn't supposed to talk to anyone or get off the bus when it made stops. I told her not to worry, that I had my golf club in case anything happened. The bus pulled out, and my sister and the baby waved good-bye.

23 Over the next 350 miles the land changed from hill country to brushland to river valley. I started getting hungry around Corpus Christi and wished that I hadn't eaten my ham and cheese sandwich before the bus left Austin. I wondered if my father would say yes to eating pizza. For a long time I imagined I was in a car on the other side of the highway, headed north instead of south. After a while, I fell asleep and then woke up just in time to see my hometown: the swaying palm trees; the fat water tower on its skinny legs, a lonely seagull hovering high above the catwalk; the bell tower at Guadalupe Church; the tamale place next to the freeway; the used-car lots, the used-car lots, the used-car lots.

24 I saw my parents standing outside the terminal. My mother was wearing her royal-blue smock from the grocery store where she worked. My father had on the straw cowboy hat that he wore for work every day. He hadn't noticed that one of his pant legs had stuck inside his boot. As soon as the door opened, my mother came up and hugged me. "How was your trip?" she asked. Then my father shook my hand and put his arm around my shoulder. When we got to the car, he put my suitcase in the trunk and told me to sit up front with him. "I hear you want pizza?" he said. I nodded. "You sure?" I nodded again.

25 Most of the lunch crowd had left by the time we got to the Pizza Hut. I slid into a wooden booth, and my parents slid into the other side. My father held on to his hat until the waitress showed him the coat hook on the edge of the booth.

26 "Would you like to see a menu or do you want the **buffet?**" the waitress asked.

27 She looked at my parents, who looked at each other for a second and then looked at me for the answer. But the truth is, I didn't exactly know what she was asking us. The word "buffet" was as foreign to me as the word "pizza" had once been.

28 "No, we just want to order pizza," I told the waitress.

29 My father nodded in approval.

30 "I'm real hungry," I said, "so I want a large pepperoni pizza. My father will eat a medium pepperoni pizza. And bring my mother a small pepperoni pizza."

31 The waitress looked up from her notepad. "You sure you don't want the buffet?" There was that word again.

32 "No, it's okay," I said. "We just want pizza."

NOTES

33   After she left, we sipped our iced teas and waited for the food. I could tell my father was proud of me for taking charge and ordering our food, the same way he would have.

34   After a while, the waitress came back and set the table. The manager helped her slide another table up against our booth. My father seemed impressed with all the work. The waitress returned a few minutes later and placed a small pepperoni pizza and then a medium one in front of my parents, leaving very little room for their plates and iced teas. My father looked at my mother when he realized how much food we had in front of us. Then the manager set a large pepperoni pizza on the extra table. "Can I get you folks anything else?" he asked.

35   I kept my head down and tried not to make eye contact with my father, which was easy, because he was busy eating more food than I'd ever seen him eat. My mother whispered to him in Spanish about this being a special lunch. To which my father answered, in English, that this would have been more special if we'd gone to a regular restaurant. Then he took a deep breath, exhaled, and continued eating. In the end, the waitress still had to bring out two boxes for the leftovers, and my mother had to dig into her purse to help my father pay for lunch.

36   After this we went back to eating the same foods. As far as I know, my parents have never entered another Italian restaurant. But me, I eat pizza wherever I go—Brooklyn, Chicago, Paris, Mexico City. If some fancy hotel has it on the menu, I know what I'm ordering. If I'm leaving a bar at two in the morning, it's nearly impossible for me to walk past an all-night pizza place. Who knows how many times I've eaten a cold slice while standing next to the refrigerator. Once, I even ordered a pizza in South America. I'd finally saved up enough money to take what I considered my first real vacation. I spent most of my time in Chile, but on New Year's Eve I caught a flight to Ushuaia, Argentina, the city at the southern tip of the continent and the world. To get there we flew over Patagonia, and the massive ice formations looked close enough to touch. Then I spotted the **elusive** straits that Magellan had discovered more than four hundred years earlier. And the land became only more distant and **remote** the farther we traveled into Tierra del Fuego. As we approached the airport in Ushuaia, the plane circled over the Beagle Channel, passing tiny islands of penguin and sea lion colonies along the way. The plane shook **desperately** against the Antarctic wind, and I thought to myself then that this was where wind was invented and here was the origin of the warm breeze we felt so far away in Brownsville. I was traveling alone and that night went out to an Italian restaurant, where I ordered a small mushroom pizza. After dinner I walked to the channel, trying to stay warm while the wind whipped around me and whistled lightly, as if someone were calling me to come closer. I stepped toward the edge of the water and pulled out a bottle of champagne I'd stashed in my jacket. An ocean liner was docked off to the side, and at midnight the crew sounded the ship's horn to mark the new year, 1994. People

NOTES

were laughing and clapping in the distance. I uncorked the champagne and took my first drink. The Andes were at my back; Antarctica was straight ahead. And the wind never stopped whistling. I stared into the darkness and wondered what else was out there.

©2005 by Oscar Casares, *Texas Monthly*, March 2005. Reproduced by permission of *Texas Monthly*.

✏ WRITE

PERSONAL RESPONSE: Do you think it's important to try new things, even if it means going against the practices of your family? What are the potential benefits and drawbacks? Is conflict likely? Write a short response to this question. Use evidence from the text to support your response.

Thank You, M'am

FICTION
Langston Hughes
1958

Introduction

Langston Hughes (1902–1967) was working as a busboy in Washington, D.C. when he showed some of his poems to famous poet Vachel Lindsay. Lindsay was so impressed that he read the poems that night to an audience. In time, Hughes became one of the first African Americans to make a living as a writer and lecturer, eventually moving back to New York and becoming a leader of the Harlem Renaissance. In Hughes's short story "Thank You, M'am," a teenage boy tries to snatch a woman's purse late one night and is surprised by what happens next.

"You ought to be my son. I would teach you right from wrong."

1 She was a large woman with a large purse that had everything in it but hammer and nails. It had a long strap, and she carried it slung across her shoulder. It was about eleven o'clock at night, and she was walking alone, when a boy ran up behind her and tried to snatch her purse. The strap broke with the single tug the boy gave it from behind. But the boy's weight and the weight of the purse combined caused him to lose his balance so, instead of taking off full blast as he had hoped, the boy fell on his back on the sidewalk, and his legs flew up. The large woman simply turned around and kicked him right square in his blue-jeaned sitter. Then she reached down, picked the boy up by his shirt front, and shook him until his teeth rattled.

2 After that the woman said, "Pick up my pocketbook, boy, and give it here." She still held him. But she bent down enough to permit him to stoop and pick up her purse. Then she said, "Now ain't you ashamed of yourself?"

3 Firmly gripped by his shirt front, the boy said, "Yes'm."

4 The woman said, "What did you want to do it for?"

5 The boy said, "I didn't aim to."

6 She said, "You a lie!"

7 By that time two or three people passed, stopped, turned to look, and some stood watching.

8 "If I turn you loose, will you run?" asked the woman.

9 "Yes'm," said the boy.

10 "Then I won't turn you loose," said the woman. She did not release him.

11 "I'm very sorry, lady, I'm sorry," whispered the boy.

12 "Um-hum! And your face is dirty. I got a great mind to wash your face for you. Ain't you got nobody home to tell you to wash your face?"

13 "No'm," said the boy.

Skill: Theme

This dialogue makes me aware of a possible theme. She asks the boy flat out if he's ashamed, which hints that the theme is developing: people should feel shame when they do something wrong.

NOTES

14　"Then it will get washed this evening," said the large woman starting up the street, dragging the frightened boy behind her.

15　He looked as if he were fourteen or fifteen, **frail** and willow-wild, in tennis shoes and blue jeans.

16　The woman said, "You ought to be my son. I would teach you right from wrong. Least I can do right now is to wash your face. Are you hungry?"

17　"No'm," said the being dragged boy. "I just want you to turn me loose."

18　"Was I bothering *you* when I turned that corner?" asked the woman.

19　"No'm."

20　"But you put yourself in **contact** with *me*," said the woman. "If you think that that contact is not going to last awhile, you got another thought coming. When I get through with you, sir, you are going to remember Mrs. Luella Bates Washington Jones."

21　Sweat popped out on the boy's face and he began to struggle. Mrs. Jones stopped, jerked him around in front of her, put a half-nelson[1] about his neck, and continued to drag him up the street. When she got to her door, she dragged the boy inside, down a hall, and into a large kitchenette-**furnished** room at the rear of the house. She switched on the light and left the door open. The boy could hear other roomers laughing and talking in the large house. Some of their doors were open, too, so he knew he and the woman were not alone. The woman still had him by the neck in the middle of her room.

22　She said, "What is your name?"

23　"Roger," answered the boy.

24　"Then, Roger, you go to that sink and wash your face," said the woman, whereupon she turned him loose—at last. Roger looked at the door—looked at the woman—looked at the door—*and went to the sink.*

25　"Let the water run until it gets warm," she said. "Here's a clean towel."

26　"You gonna take me to jail?" asked the boy, bending over the sink.

27　"Not with that face, I would not take you nowhere," said the woman. "Here I am trying to get home to cook me a bite to eat and you snatch my pocketbook! Maybe, you ain't been to your supper either, late as it be. Have you?"

28　"There's nobody home at my house," said the boy.

1.　**half-nelson** a wrestling hold of an opponent's neck

Skill: Media

In the filmed version of this part, the camera focuses on Roger's face. He looks embarrassed and sad. Maybe he feels some regret?

In the film, we also see Mrs. Jones get down to Roger's level to talk to him. This angle emphasizes what she's saying: his actions have consequences. Maybe this has to do with the story's meaning. She seems to be really trying to communicate with him.

Skill:
Media

The camera focuses on Roger, and he yells, "M'am?" This makes me think he's shocked by Mrs. Jones's statement. Roger doesn't seem so shocked in the written version.

This part is also different from the story. Roger throws the towel on the ground but then picks it up. I think he realizes that the lady has been nice to him, so he should treat her things with respect. This might have something do with the theme.

29   "Then we'll eat," said the woman, "I believe you're hungry—or been hungry—to try to snatch my pocketbook."

30   "I wanted a pair of blue suede shoes," said the boy.

31   "Well, you didn't have to snatch *my* pocketbook to get some suede shoes," said Mrs. Luella Bates Washington Jones. "You could of asked me."

32   "M'am?"

33   The water dripping from his face, the boy looked at her. There was a long pause. A very long pause. After he had dried his face and not knowing what else to do dried it again, the boy turned around, wondering what next. The door was open. He could make a dash for it down the hall. He could run, run, run, run, *run!*

34   The woman was sitting on the day-bed. After a while she said, "I were young once and I wanted things I could not get."

35   There was another long pause. The boy's mouth opened. Then he frowned, but not knowing he frowned.

36   The woman said, "Um-hum! You thought I was going to say *but*, didn't you? You thought I was going to say, *but I didn't snatch people's pocketbooks.* Well, I wasn't going to say that." Pause. Silence. "I have done things, too, which I would not tell you, son—neither tell God, if he didn't already know. So you set down while I fix us something to eat. You might run that comb through your hair so you will look **presentable.**"

37   In another corner of the room behind a screen was a gas plate[2] and an icebox[3]. Mrs. Jones got up and went behind the screen. The woman did not watch the boy to see if he was going to run now, nor did she watch her purse which she left behind her on the day-bed. But the boy took care to sit on the far side of the room where he thought she could easily see him out of the corner of her eye, if she wanted to. He did not trust the woman *not* to trust him. And he did not want to be **mistrusted** now.

38   "Do you need somebody to go to the store," asked the boy, "maybe to get some milk or something?"

39   "Don't believe I do," said the woman, "unless you just want sweet milk yourself. I was going to make cocoa out of this canned milk I got here."

40   "That will be fine," said the boy.

---

2. **gas plate** a small appliance for cooking
3. **icebox** appliances used to keep food cold prior to the invention of modern refrigerators

41 She heated some lima beans and ham she had in the icebox, made the cocoa, and set the table. The woman did not ask the boy anything about where he lived, or his folks, or anything else that would embarrass him. Instead, as they ate, she told him about her job in a hotel beauty-shop that stayed open late, what the work was like, and how all kinds of women came in and out, blondes, red-heads, and Spanish. Then she cut him a half of her ten-cent cake.

42 "Eat some more, son," she said.

43 When they were finished eating she got up and said, "Now, here, take this ten dollars and buy yourself some blue suede shoes. And next time, do not make the mistake of latching onto *my* pocketbook *nor nobody else's*—because shoes come by devilish like that will burn your feet. I got to get my rest now. But I wish you would behave yourself, son, from here on in."

44 She led him down the hall to the front door and opened it. "Good-night! Behave yourself, boy!" she said, looking out into the street.

45 The boy wanted to say something else other than "Thank you, m'am" to Mrs. Luella Bates Washington Jones, but he couldn't do so as he turned at the barren stoop[4] and looked back at the large woman in the door. He barely managed to say "Thank you" before she shut the door. And he never saw her again.

"Thank You, M'am" from SHORT STORIES by Langston Hughes. Copyright © 1996 by Ramona Bass and Arnold Rampersad. Reprinted by permission of Hill and Wang, a division of Farrar, Straus and Giroux, LLC.

4. **stoop** a porch, entryway steps, or platform at the entrance to a house

First Read

Read "Thank You, M'am." After you read, complete the Think Questions below.

☁ THINK QUESTIONS

1. How do Roger and Mrs. Luella Bates Washington Jones first meet? What is Mrs. Jones's immediate reaction to this event? Cite specific evidence from the text to support your response.

2. Rather than call the police, what does Mrs. Jones do to Roger? How does Roger initially respond? Cite specific evidence from the text to support your analysis.

3. What reason does Roger give Mrs. Jones for why he tried to snatch her pocketbook? What is one thing Mrs. Jones says in response? How do her words affect him? Cite specific evidence from the text to support your statements.

4. Find the word **contact** in paragraph 20 of "Thank You, M'am." Use context clues in the surrounding sentences, as well as the sentence in which the word appears, to determine the word's meaning. Write your definition here, and identify clues that helped you figure out its meaning.

5. Use context clues to determine the meaning of **presentable** as it is used in paragraph 36 of "Thank You, M'am." Write your definition here, and identify clues that helped you figure out the meaning. Then check the meaning in a dictionary.

Skill:
Media

Use the Checklist to analyze Media in "Thank You, M'am." Refer to the sample student annotations about Media in the text.

••• CHECKLIST FOR MEDIA

In order to determine how to compare and contrast a written story, drama, or poem to its audio, filmed, staged, or multimedia version, do the following:

✓ choose a story that has been presented in multiple forms of media, such as a written story and a film adaptation

✓ note techniques that are unique to each medium—print, audio, and video:

- lighting
- sound
- color
- tone and style
- camera focus and angles
- word choice
- structure

✓ examine how these techniques may have an effect on the story and its ideas, as well as the reader's, listener's, or viewer's understanding of the work as a whole

✓ examine similarities and differences between the written story and its audio or video versions

Please note that excerpts and passages in the StudySync® library and this workbook are intended as touchstones to generate interest in an author's work. The excerpts and passages do not substitute for the reading of entire texts, and StudySync® strongly recommends that students seek out and purchase the whole literary or informational work in order to experience it as the author intended. Links to online resellers are available in our digital library. In addition, complete works may be ordered through an authorized reseller by filling out and returning to StudySync® the order form enclosed in this workbook.

Reading & Writing Companion   105

To compare and contrast a written story, drama, or poem to its audio, filmed, staged, or multimedia version, analyzing the effects of techniques unique to each medium, consider the following questions:

- ✓ How do different types of media treat story elements?

- ✓ What techniques are unique to each medium—print, audio, and video?

- ✓ How does the medium—for example, a film's use of music, sound, and camera angles—affect a person's understanding of the work as a whole?

Skill:
Media

Reread paragraphs 34–36 of "Thank You, M'am." Then, using the Checklist on the previous page, answer the multiple-choice questions below.

🔁 YOUR TURN

1. This question has two parts. First, answer Part A. Then, answer Part B.

   Part A: Which of the following details in "Thank You, M'am" is different in the filmed version from the written story?

   ○ A. Mrs. Jones asked Roger to wash his hands to make himself presentable for dinner.

   ○ B. Roger asks Mrs. Jones what kinds of bad things she did when she was his age.

   ○ C. Mrs. Jones admits that she also has done bad things.

   ○ D. Mrs. Jones says, "Everyone has something in common."

   Part B: Which of the following BEST explains the effect of the change detailed in Part A?

   ○ A. The added line suggests a theme that people are connected even though they are different.

   ○ B. The added line helps Roger see that he really should comb his hair.

   ○ C. Mrs. Jones needed to make it clear to Roger that she and his mother have a lot in common.

   ○ D. The added line suggests Roger is related to Mrs. Jones.

2. This question has two parts. First, answer Part A. Then, answer Part B.

   Part A: What film element is added to the scene to enhance the meaning or message?

   ○ A. In the film we see that they're both eating, but in the text, she hasn't made the meal yet.

   ○ B. The film keeps both characters on the screen the whole time.

   ○ C. Mrs. Jones pats Roger on the head as the camera follows her from the couch to the hall.

   ○ D. The camera focuses on Roger's eye roll when Mrs. Jones says everyone has something in common.

Part B: How does the film element added in Part A affect the meaning or message of the story?

○ A. The head pat shows Mrs. Jones relates to Roger and suggests a message about forgiveness.

○ B. The food in the scene emphasizes that food brings people together.

○ C. The scene shows that Roger and Mrs. Jones are connected even though they just met.

○ D. Roger rolling his eyes shows us that he isn't ready to be good yet.

Skill:
Theme

Use the Checklist to analyze Theme in "Thank You, M'am." Refer to the sample student annotations about Theme in the text.

••• CHECKLIST FOR THEME

In order to identify a theme or central idea in a text and analyze its development over the course of the text, note the following:

✓ the topic of the text

✓ whether or not the theme is stated directly in the text

✓ details in the text that help to reveal theme

- • a narrator's or speaker's tone

- • title and chapter headings

- • details about the setting

- • characters' thoughts, actions, and dialogue

- • the central conflict in the story's plot

- • the resolution of the conflict

- • whether or not the theme is stated directly in the text

✓ analyze how characters and the problems they face are affected by the setting and what impact this may have on how the theme is developed

To determine a theme or central idea of a text and analyze its development over the course of the text, consider the following questions:

✓ What is a theme, or central idea, of the text?

✓ When did you become aware of that theme? For instance, did the story's conclusion reveal the theme?

✓ How does the theme develop over the course of the text?

Skill:
Theme

Reread paragraphs 8–14 of "Thank You, M'am." Then, using the Checklist on the previous page, answer the multiple-choice questions below.

YOUR TURN

1. Based on Mrs. Jones's dialogue in paragraphs 12 and 14, the reader can infer that—

   ○ A. Mrs. Jones cares more about appearance than character.
   ○ B. Mrs. Jones is a tough but caring person.
   ○ C. Mrs. Jones plans on taking Roger to the police station after he cleans up.
   ○ D. Mrs. Jones has little sympathy for Roger.

2. Roger's responses in paragraphs 9, 11, and 13 reveal that he—

   ○ A. has no regret for attempting to steal Mrs. Jones's purse.
   ○ B. is planning to kick Mrs. Jones as soon as she lets her guard down.
   ○ C. is clever and wants Mrs. Jones to feel sorry for him so that she lets him go.
   ○ D. shows signs of honesty and likely has a tough life with little guidance from adults.

3. The dialogue in paragraphs 12 through 14 hints that the theme might be—

   ○ A. Sometimes it is important to notice other people's struggles and offer help.
   ○ B. The way you look often reflects the way you feel.
   ○ C. In some cases, the only way to teach a lesson is through fear.
   ○ D. It's important to make a positive first impression.

Close Read

THANK YOU, M'AM

Reread "Thank You, M'am." As you reread, complete the Skills Focus questions below. Then use your answers and annotations from the questions to help you complete the Write activity.

◎ SKILLS FOCUS

1. Identify parts in the story where Mrs. Jones shows concern about Roger's dirty face and hunger. Explain what message the story might be expressing about self-respect.

2. Reread paragraphs 34–36. Identify details that suggest why Mrs. Jones may be helping Roger. Explain what theme, or message about life, is hinted at in these paragraphs.

3. Identify details that may explain why Mrs. Jones gives Roger money to buy blue suede shoes. Explain whether you agree or disagree with her decision and whether you think Roger should have accepted the money.

4. "Mad," "In the Year 1974," and "Thank You, M'am" all deal with clashes between young and old. Identify textual evidence in "Thank You, M'am" that reveals a lesson Mrs. Jones is trying to teach Roger. Explain how that passage compares and contrasts with one of the other pieces.

5. Identify parts in the story where you were surprised by how either Mrs. Jones or Roger responds to the early conflict between the two characters. Explain why the character's actions surprised you and what you expected instead.

✏ WRITE

COMPARE AND CONTRAST: "Thank You, M'am," "In the Year 1974," and "Mad" are about conflicts between young people and older adults. What lessons are learned in each text as a result of these conflicts? Compare and contrast the lesson in "Thank You, M'am" to the lesson in one of the other texts. Remember to support your ideas with evidence from the texts.

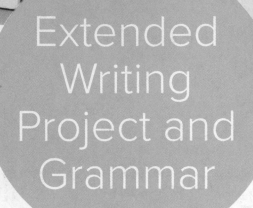

Extended Writing Project and Grammar

EXTENDED
WRITING
PROJECT

NARRATIVE
WRITING

Narrative Writing Process: Plan

| PLAN | DRAFT | REVISE | EDIT AND PUBLISH |

Conflict drives stories. Conflict gives characters a purpose and gives readers a reason to care about them. Some conflicts are straightforward: Rikki-tikki-tavi must defeat Nag and Nagaina. Other conflicts are less obvious. In "Seventh Grade," Victor's desire to impress Teresa leads him to lie about being able to speak French. Sources for conflict can seem endless, but determining a conflict early on in your planning can help you figure out your other story elements: character, plot, setting, and theme.

WRITING PROMPT

What conflicts would exist in a world where people can know what others are thinking?

Imagine a world where people can know what others are thinking. What conflicts would cease to exist in that world? What new conflicts would arise? Write a story about a conflict that exists because it's possible to know another person's thoughts. Regardless of the conflict you choose, be sure your narrative includes the following:

- a plot with a beginning, middle, and end
- a clear setting
- characters and dialogue
- a distinct conflict
- a clear theme

Introduction to Narrative Writing

Narrative writing tells a story of experiences or events that have been imagined by a writer or that have happened in real life. Good fiction writing uses effective techniques, relevant descriptive details, and a purposeful structure with a series of events that contain a beginning, middle, and end. The characteristics of fiction writing include:

- setting
- characters
- plot
- theme
- point of view

As you continue with this Extended Writing Project, you'll receive more instruction and practice at crafting each of the characteristics of fiction writing to create your own narrative story.

Before you get started on your own narrative, read this narrative that one student, Jalyn, wrote in response to the writing prompt. As you read the Model, highlight and annotate the features of narrative writing that Jalyn included in her narrative.

Copyright © BookheadEd Learning, LLC

NOTES

☰ STUDENT MODEL

The Talent Show

1   Anh Le was good at music, but she was even better at something else. She could hear people's thoughts. She kept it a secret because it was the only way to figure out what went on in people's heads. But sometimes it was more of a curse than a blessing.

2   Like when she quit taking piano lessons, her mother had complained loudly, "How can you waste your natural gift?" *After all that money spent on lessons,* she had thought.

3   But Anh still loved music, and she kept playing every day. When she started middle school, she joined the choir. It became her favorite school activity. She and her friends had fun pretending to be reality-show singers on weekends, using a karaoke machine that belonged to Jennifer's family. Jen's dad was so impressed that he suggested they enter a competition at their local community center. There would be a preliminary round in one month and a final round the following week.

4   The prize was a free ticket to the new amusement park! Anh and her brother had been begging her parents to go since before it opened.

5   "Which song do you think I should sing?" Anh asked. *Which one will make me the winner?* she thought.

6   "I think you should try 'Hero,'" Jennifer said distractedly. She was thinking about riding the spiralling roller coaster.

7   "Yeah, or maybe 'Tonight,'" Valeria added. *How much cotton candy can I eat if I win?*

8   "You two should do a duet," Anh suggested. Their voices went well together. *And my chances to win are probably higher if I do a solo. But then again, they can practice with the karaoke machine.*

9   "We're all going to do great! They'll have to split first place three ways," Jennifer and Valeria said together.

10 Anh realized her friends didn't care about the music as much as she did. They were really just interested in the tickets. She decided that she needed to work hard to beat them.

11 She knew her brother Thao would play the piano for her to practice. She'd just have to make him those peanut butter cookies he'd been thinking about all week. She baked enough to keep him going before the first round of the competition.

12 Soon enough, the big day came. Anh did her warm-up exercises after breakfast in her bedroom. *I'm gonna nail this,* she told herself as she headed downstairs. In the kitchen she heard her brother trying to convince their parents that he couldn't go to the competition. "I feel sick," he said. *I haven't played ANY video games in weeks because of her practicing,* he thought. *I'd rather stay home and do that.* Anh smirked when she realized she'd be on all those rides at the park before Thao. *I'm gonna win. He can sit at home and play video games.*

13 She turned her attention back to the competition. She wanted the right kind of energy to keep the judges awake. She planned to wow them.

14 But when she got to the auditorium, Anh was overwhelmed with nerves. She felt butterflies in her stomach, her mouth was dry, and she could only hear her heart. *What if I forget the words? Or worse, what if I open my mouth and forget how to sing?*

15 *. . . Who are all these newbies?* She heard a competitor thinking. *I'll have no problem taking the trophy home again this year . . .*

16 *. . . We got this!* This time it was Valeria. *Our practice last night came out perfectly . . .*

17 Anh found a quiet area backstage to take some deep breaths. *I know this song,* she thought. *I could actually sing it in my sleep.*

18 When she went onstage, Anh was determined to give it her all. She felt the bright spotlights shining down on her, the crowd got silent, and she could hear the judges tapping their pencils and moving

their papers. She took a deep breath and felt the butterflies in her stomach disappear. As she started to sing, she was able to forget her nervousness and focus on the lyrics. She stood taller and felt even more confident. She didn't miss a single beat! The crowd applauded loudly. Next, the judges weighed in.

19   "I like the emotion you put into it," said one judge dryly. He was an older man in a worn-out suit. *I hope this is over soon . . . I could really go for a steak burrito right now.*

20   Anh managed a half smile and braced herself for the next judge.

21   "You have a nice voice," the young woman said. *This is the last time I do a favor for my sister. If she's going to make us work all day, she needs to pay us!*

22   *. . . She did her best. But we're gonna do even better.* Anh heard Valeria's thoughts drift into her own. She knew she was gonna have to try harder next round. If she made it.

23   After the competition Valeria and Jennifer had already started thinking about choosing their next song. *Should it be a pop song or a classic? How high IS the roller coaster, anyway? I heard a ninth grader already set a record for riding it the most times in one hour . . .*

24   But Anh scored high, and so did Valeria and Jennifer. At the end of the competition they all made it to the second round.

25   The following week, Anh sang with more energy than before, and grinned at her brother from the stage. *I can't wait to see the look on his face when I tell him about all those water slides . . .* she thought as she finished her song.

26   "Another excellent performance. Nice range of emotion," the judge said flatly. He was wearing the same worn suit and thinking about his heartburn.

27   Anh tried hard not to roll her eyes.

28   "You control your voice well," the second judge said. "Lots of nice touches in that song." *At least she was on key this time.*

29   Anh swallowed. *I guess that's a good thing, right?*

Extended Writing Project and Grammar

30   Anh lined up on the stage with the rest of the contestants at the end of the day, crossing her fingers as she waited to hear her name announced in first place. She wanted to win so badly, and she had practiced so hard for the entire month before the competition! She had been so focused on the music and she remembered how her friends had only really cared about the tickets. She had given it her all!

31   But to her dismay (and the dismay of the previous winner), it was Valeria and Jennifer who took home the trophy. Anh was disappointed to be in second place, but at least she knew her friends would tell her all about the park's rides.

32   *I wish Anh could come with us*, she heard them both think.

Please note that excerpts and passages in the StudySync® library and this workbook are intended as touchstones to generate interest in an author's work. The excerpts and passages do not substitute for the reading of entire texts, and StudySync® strongly recommends that students seek out and purchase the whole literary or informational work in order to experience it as the author intended. Links to online resellers are available in our digital library. In addition, complete works may be ordered through an authorized reseller by filling out and returning to StudySync® the order form enclosed in this workbook.

Reading & Writing
Companion

117

✏ WRITE

Writers often take notes about story ideas before they sit down to write. Think about what you've learned so far about organizing narrative writing to help you begin prewriting.

- **Genre:** In what sort of genre would you like to write? Most any genre can focus on a conflict. Genres include realistic fiction, science fiction, fantasy, or mystery, to name some examples.

- **Characters:** What types of characters would you like to write about in your narrative?

- **Conflict/Theme:** What conflict will you make your characters deal with? What life lesson will your characters or readers learn from the conflict?

- **Setting:** How might the setting of your story affect the characters and problem?

- **Plot:** What events will lead to the resolution of the conflict while keeping a reader engaged?

- **Point of View:** From which point of view should your story be told, and why?

Response Instructions

Use the questions in the bulleted list to write a one-paragraph summary. Your summary should describe what will happen in your narrative like the one above.

Don't worry about including all of the details now. Focus only on the most essential and important elements. You will refer back to this short summary as you continue through the steps of the writing process.

Skill:
Organizing Narrative Writing

••• CHECKLIST FOR ORGANIZING NARRATIVE WRITING

As you consider how to organize your narrative, use the following questions as a guide:

- Who is the narrator and who are the characters in the story?
- From what point of view will the story be told?
- Where will the story take place?
- What conflict or problem will the characters have to resolve?
- Does my plot flow logically and naturally from one event to the next?

Here are some strategies to help you organize your narrative so the event sequence unfolds naturally and logically:

- Introduce the characters and/or a narrator.

  > Characters can be introduced all at once or throughout the narrative.

  > Choose the role each character will play.

  > Choose a point of view.

    o A first-person narrator can be a participant or character in the story.

    o A third-person narrator tells the story as an outside observer.

- Outline the five stages of plot development.

  > Begin with your **exposition**—decide what background information your readers need to know about the characters, setting, and conflict.

  > List the events of the **rising action**—be sure that these events build toward the climax.

  > Describe what will happen during the **climax** of the story—make sure that this is the point of highest interest, conflict, or suspense in your story.

  > List the events of the **falling action**—make sure that these events show what happens to the characters as a result of the climax.

  > Explain the **resolution**—make sure the main conflict is solved or settled.

Copyright © BookheadEd Learning, LLC

⟳ YOUR TURN

Complete the chart below by placing the student notes and ideas in the correct part of the outline.

	Student Notes and Ideas Options
A	As Karl campaigns, he starts to feel self-conscious. One day, he feels everyone staring at him. Suddenly, he hears what everyone is thinking. He learns that no one really likes him.
B	My main character is Karl. Other characters include his classmates.
C	Karl runs for class president. He is popular, but is self-centered and mean to many less-popular students. Karl doesn't listen to them and thinks they are worthless, but everyone is scared to confront him about this.
D	Karl stops hearing everyone's thoughts. But now he understands people better and listens to them.
E	Karl loses a close race for class president. He is relieved.
F	The story will be told by an outside narrator, or third-person point of view.
G	At the final debate, Karl addresses the whole student crowd. He apologizes for being mean and says he will change.

Part of the Outline	Student Notes and Ideas
Characters	
Narrator	
Exposition	
Rising Action	
Climax	
Falling Action	
Resolution	

↻ YOUR TURN

Plan your narrative story by completing the outline. You may refer to the checklist section as you write.

Part of the Outline	Notes and Ideas
Characters	
Narrator	
Exposition	
Rising Action	
Climax	
Falling Action	
Resolution	

Narrative Writing Process: Draft

| PLAN | DRAFT | REVISE | EDIT AND PUBLISH |

You have already made progress toward writing your short story. Now it is time to draft your narrative.

✎ WRITE

Use your plan and other responses in your Binder to draft your narrative. You may also have new ideas as you begin drafting. Feel free to explore those new ideas as you have them. You can also ask yourself these questions:

- Have I included specifics about my setting, characters, plot, theme, and point of view?
- Have I made my conflict clear to the reader?
- Does the sequence of events in my story make sense?

Before you submit your draft, read it over carefully. You want to be sure that you've responded to all aspects of the prompt.

Here is Jalyn's short story draft. As you read, identify details that Jalyn includes in her exposition. Because this is a draft, there are some errors that Jalyn will revise as she works toward her final version.

≡ STUDENT MODEL: FIRST DRAFT

~~Anh Le was good at music but she knew what people thought. she didn't tell anyone that though.~~

~~Anh started taking piano lessons when she was seven. She quit and her mom got mad.~~

Anh Le was good at music, but she was even better at something else. She could hear people's thoughts. She kept it a secret because it was the only way to figure out what went on in people's heads. But sometimes it was more of a curse than a blessing.

Like when she quit taking piano lessons, her mother had complained loudly, "How can you waste your natural gift?" *After all that money spent on lessons,* she had thought.

But anh still loved music. When she started middle school she joined the choir. It became her favorite school activity. She and her friends had fun pretending to be reality-show singers on weekends, using a karaoke machine that belonged to Jennifer's family. Jen's dad was so impresed that he suggested they enter a local competition. There would be a prelimenary round in one month and a final round the following week.

The friends looked online, found a competition at a nearby community center. The competition was open to kids.

~~"Which song do you think I should sing" Anh asked. She wanted to win.~~

~~"I think you should try 'Hero,'" Jennifer said distractedly.~~

~~So did Valeria. "Whatever." In her head she thought, "How much cotton candy can I eat if I win?"~~

~~Anh thinks they should sing a duet because their voices were good together. She was thinking about how she might have a better~~

Skill: Story Beginnings

Jalyn writes an exciting opening to better engage and orient the reader. She wants to grab the reader's attention with Anh's unique talent. She also wants to give the reader more context.

chance to win with a solo. Then she remembered the karaoke machine. She decided she needed to work hard to beat them.

"We're all going to do great! They'll have to split first place three ways," they said together.

Anh realizd her friends didn't care about the music as much as she did. They were really just interested in the tickets. She decided that she needed to work hard to beat them.

"Which song do you think I should sing?" Anh asked. *Which one will make me the winner?* she thought.

"I think you should try 'Hero,'" Jennifer said distractedly. She was thinking about riding the spiralling roller coaster.

"Yeah, or maybe 'Tonight,'" Valeria added. *How much cotton candy can I eat if I win?*

"You two should do a duet," Anh suggested. Their voices went well together. *And my chances to win are probably higher if I do a solo. But then again, they can practice with the karaoke machine.*

"We're all going to do great! They'll have to split first place three ways," Jennifer and Valeria said together.

Anh realized her friends didn't care about the music as much as she did. They were really just interested in the tickets. She decided that she needed to work hard to beat them.

She knew her brother Thao would play the piano for her to practice. She'd just have to make him those Peanut Butter cookies he'd been thinking about all week. She baked enough, to keep him going before the first round of the competition.

Soon enough, the big day came. Anh did her warm-up excersises after breakfast. she told herself she was gonna win. When she headed downstairs she heard her brother trying to convince their parents that he couldn't go to the competition. "I feel sick," he said. I haven't played ANY video games in weeks because of her practicing, he thought. He wanted to stay home for that instead. Anh was happy

Skill: Narrative Techniques

Jalyn first decides to write new dialogue to further develop the experiences, events, and characters. She adds dialogue to increase conflict and lead readers from one plot event to the next. She includes dialogue tags so readers can understand which characters are speaking.

~~when she realized she'd be on all those rides at the park before Thao. I'm gonna win. He can sit at home and play video games.~~

Soon enough, the big day came. Anh did her warm-up exercises after breakfast in her bedroom. *I'm gonna nail this*, she told herself as she headed downstairs. In the kitchen she heard her brother trying to convince their parents that he couldn't go to the competition. "I feel sick," he said. *I haven't played ANY video games in weeks because of her practicing,* he thought. *I'd rather stay home and do that.* Anh smirked when she realized she'd be on all those rides at the park before Thao. *I'm gonna win. He can sit at home and play video games.*

She turned her attention back to the competition. She wanted the right kind of energy to keep the judges awake. She planned to do a good job.

But when she got to the auditorium, Anh was overwhelmed with nerves. What if I forget the words? Or worse, what if I open my mouth and forget how to sing?

The other competitores and their parents were all thinking nervously. Who are all these newbys? She heard a competitor thinking. I'll have no problem taking the trophy home again this year . . .

. . . We got this! This time it was valeria. Our practice last night came out perfectly . . .

Anh found a quiet area backstage to take some deep breaths. I know this song, she thought. I could actually sing it in my sleep.

~~Anh was able to forget her nervousness and focus on the lyrics when she started to sing. As she walked out on stage, she was determined to give it her all. The crowd clapped, and then it was time for the two judges to talk.~~

~~"I like the emotion you put into it," said the first judge. Anh heard his thoughts, "i hope this is over soon. I'm hungry. I want a steak burrito. There needs to be some dancing to go with all this singing.~~

 Skill:
Transitions

Jalyn decides to use transition words to signal shifts in the setting as Anh moves around her house. Phrases like "in her bedroom" and "as she headed downstairs" help the reader visualize Anh and signal shifts in the setting as the plot flows.

NOTES

⚙ Skill:
Descriptive
Details

Jalyn adds more descriptive details and precise language to her draft. Descriptive details such as "an older man in a worn-out suit" help readers imagine what Anh sees. Adding "The crowd applauded loudly" conveys the exact volume level of the audience.

~~The other judge, a young woman who looked like a singer herself, said, "You have a nice voice." However she really thought, "Too bad it's a little off-key.~~

As she started to sing, she was able to forget her nervousness and focus on the lyrics. She stood taller and felt even more confident. She didn't miss a single beat! The crowd applauded loudly. Next, the judges weighed in.

"I like the emotion you put into it," said one judge dryly. He was an older man in a worn-out suit. *I hope this is over soon . . . I could really go for a steak burrito right now.*

Anh managed a half smile and braced herself for the next judge.

"You have a nice voice," the young woman said. *This is the last time I do a favor for my sister. If she's going to make us work all day, she needs to pay us!*

. . . She did her best. But we're gonna do even better. Anh heard valeria's thoughts. She knew she was gonna have to try harder next round. If she made it.

Valeria and Jennifer had already started thinking about choosing their next song. *Should it be a Pop song or a Classic? How high IS the roller coaster, anyway? I heard a ninth grader already set a record for riding it the most times in one hour . . .*

But Anh scored high, and so did Valeria and Jennifer. They all scored high enough to made it to the second round so they could come back next week.

The following week, Anh was singing with more energy than before, and grinned at her brother from the stage. *I can't wait to see the look on his face when I tell him about all those water slides . . .*

"Another excellent performance. Nice range of emotion," the Judge said flatly. *He was wearing that suit and thinking about his heartburn.*

Anh tried hard not to roll her eyes.

"You control your voice well," the second Judge said. "Lots of nice touches in that song." She was thinking that maybe Anh was a little less off-key this time. Definitely less off-key than the boy before her.

Anh swallowed. I guess that's a good thin, right?

~~Anh lined up on the stage with the rest of the contestants at the end of the day and she was crossing her fingers as she waited to hear her name announced in first place so she could be the winner and get the tickets. She had practiced so hard! But to her dismay (and the dismay of the previous winner) it was Valeria and Jennifer who took home the Trophy. Anh was disappointed to be in second place, but at least she knew her friends would tell her all about the park's rides.~~

~~She heard them both think. and they weren't even being fake about it. They were thinking positive thoughts because they meant it.~~

Anh lined up on the stage with the rest of the contestants at the end of the day, crossing her fingers as she waited to hear her name announced in first place. She wanted to win so badly, and she had practiced so hard for the entire month before the competition! She had been so focused on the music and she remembered how her friends had only really cared about the tickets. She had given it her all!

But to her dismay (and the dismay of the previous winner), it was Valeria and Jennifer who took home the trophy. Anh was disappointed to be in second place, but at least she knew her friends would tell her all about the park's rides.

I wish Anh could come with us, she heard them both think.

Anh smiled. I'm glad that my secret talent shows me who my real freinds are.

She watched them gigling and posing for the photographer. She knew she could convince her mom to get her a ticket to the park— she'd just heard her thinking about buying Anh a day pass. And her brother was even going to let her win a few video games.

Skill:
Conclusions

To make her draft stronger, Jalyn decides to do three things. First, she includes more character thoughts and feelings. Second, she works in important details to help summarize the main events. Third, she adds a line to reveal why the story matters.

. . . Although she'd probably have won if she kept up the piano! She heard her mother think. Anh started to laugh and, walked towards her family who were waiting for her backstage.

"What's so funny?" her brother asked, surprised at her laughter.

"Nothing, punching his shoulder lightly. She was gonna enjoy it when he let her win because he didn't know that she could read his mind because of her secret talent.

Skill:
Story Beginnings

••• CHECKLIST FOR STORY BEGINNINGS

Before you write the beginning of your narrative, ask yourself the following questions:

- What information does my reader need to know at the beginning of the story about the narrator, main character, setting, and the character's conflict?

- What will happen to my character in the story?

- Who is the narrator of my story?

There are many ways you can engage and orient your reader. Here are some strategies to help you establish a context, show the point of view, and introduce the narrator and/or characters:

- Action

  > Instead of beginning with a description of a character, have the character "doing something" that will reveal his or her personality.

  > Opening a story with an immediate conflict can help grab a reader's attention.

- Description

  > Use engaging or interesting description to establish the character, setting, or conflict.

- Dialogue

  > Dialogue can immediately establish the point of view in a story.

    o first person: narrator is a character in the story

    o third person: narrator is outside the story

- A character's internal thoughts can provide information that only the reader knows.

⟳ YOUR TURN

Read the beginning of each story below. Then, complete the chart by writing the story beginning strategy that correctly matches each paragraph.

Strategy Options		
Action	Description	Dialogue

Story Beginning	Strategy
He was a mongoose, rather like a little cat in his fur and his tail, but quite like a weasel in his head and his habits. His eyes and the end of his restless nose were pink. He could scratch himself anywhere he pleased with any leg, front or back, that he chose to use. "Rikki-Tikki-Tavi"	
"I have no use for old people in my village," he said haughtily. "They are neither useful nor able to work for a living. I therefore decree that anyone over seventy-one must be banished from the village and left in the mountains to die." "The Wise Old Woman"	
It was about eleven o'clock at night, and she was walking alone, when a boy ran up behind her and tried to snatch her purse. "Thank You, M'am"	

✎ WRITE

Use the questions and techniques in the checklist section to revise the beginning of your narrative.

Skill:
Descriptive Details

First, reread the draft of your narrative and identify the following:

- where descriptive details are needed to convey experiences and events

- vague, general, or overused words and phrases

- places where you want to tell how something looks, sounds, feels, smells, or tastes, such as:

  > experiences

  > events

  > action

Use precise words and phrases, relevant descriptive details, and sensory language to capture the action and convey experiences and events, using the following questions as a guide:

- What experiences and events do I want to convey in my writing?

- Have I included relevant and descriptive details?

- Where can I add descriptive details to describe the characters and the events of the plot?

- How can I use sensory language, or words that describe sights, sounds, feelings, smells, or tastes, to help my reader create a picture of the action, experiences, and events?

- What can I refine or revise in my word choice to make sure that the reader can picture what is taking place?

↻ YOUR TURN

Choose the best answer to each question.

1. Jalyn would like to add a descriptive sound detail to this sentence from a previous draft. Which sentence BEST adds sound detail to her sentence?

> She watched her friends posing for the photographer.

- ○ A. She watched her friends posing and giggling for the photographer as the camera snapped and clicked.
- ○ B. She watched her friends posing for the photographer, the bland dryness of her mouth reminding her of the song she had just worked so hard to sing.
- ○ C. Inhaling the celebratory scent of flowers given to her by her parents still was not enough to make Anh feel like a winner as she watched her friends posing for the photographer.
- ○ D. She watched her friends posing for the photographer, their trophy shining and sparkling under the lights above the stage.

2. Jalyn would like to add some detail. Which sentence could BEST follow and provide support for the underlined sentence in the paragraph below?

> Anh turned her attention back to the competition. She wanted the right kind of energy to keep the judges awake. <u>She planned to wow them.</u>

- ○ A. She breathed in the scent of popcorn that someone in the front row was loudly chewing.
- ○ B. She heard one judge turn the page of his notebook as he prepared to jot down notes for each performer.
- ○ C. The judges would hear the smooth sound of her voice and have no choice but to announce her the winner.
- ○ D. She felt the bright lights on her face as sweat began to form on the palms of her hands.

⟳ YOUR TURN

Complete the chart by writing a descriptive detail that appeals to each sense for your narrative.

Sense	Descriptive Detail
Sight	
Smell	
Touch	
Taste	
Sound	

Skill:
Narrative Techniques

••• CHECKLIST FOR NARRATIVE TECHNIQUES

As you begin to develop the techniques you will use in your narrative, ask yourself the following questions:

- Which characters are talking? How am I organizing the dialogue?

- How quickly or slowly do I want the plot to move? Why?

- Which literary devices can be added to strengthen the characters or plot? How can I better engage the reader?

There are many techniques you can use in a narrative. Here are some methods that can help you write dialogue, pacing, and description to develop experiences, events, and/or characters:

- Use dialogue between characters to explain events or move the action forward.

  > Set all spoken dialogue off in quotation marks, using name tags as needed.

  > Italicize internal thoughts, using identifying name tags as needed.

- Include description to engage the reader and help him or her visualize the characters, setting, and other elements in the narrative.

  > Include only those descriptions relevant to the reader's understanding of the element being described.

  > Consider using literary devices or figurative language such as imagery, metaphors, similes, personification, or idioms.

- Use pacing effectively to convey a sense of urgency or calm in a narrative.

  > To speed up the pace, try using limited description, short paragraphs, brief dialogue, and simpler sentences.

  > To slow down the pace, try using detailed description, longer paragraphs, and more complex sentence structures.

- Use any combination of the above narrative techniques to develop experiences, events, and/or characters.

↻ YOUR TURN

Read each excerpt below. Then, complete the chart by writing the narrative technique that correctly matches each paragraph.

Narrative Technique Options		
Dialogue	Pacing	Description

Excerpt	Excerpt Narrative Technique
"I mean if she's real, she's in big trouble. How long do you think somebody who's really like that is going to last around here?" *Stargirl*	
Then Rikki-tikki went out into the garden to see what was to be seen. It was a large garden, only half cultivated, with bushes, as big as summer-houses, of Marshal Niel roses, lime and orange trees, clumps of bamboos, and thickets of high grass. Rikki-tikki licked his lips. "This is a splendid hunting-ground," he said, and his tail grew bottle-brushy at the thought of it, and he scuttled up and down the garden, snuffing here and there till he heard very sorrowful voices in a thorn-bush. "Rikki-Tikki-Tavi"	
Sweat popped out on the boy's face and he began to struggle. Mrs. Jones stopped, jerked him around in front of her, put a half-nelson about his neck, and continued to drag him up the street. When she got to her door, she dragged the boy inside, down a hall, and into a large kitchenette-furnished room at the rear of the house. She switched on the light and left the door open. The boy could hear other roomers laughing and talking in the large house. "Thank You, M'am"	

♻ YOUR TURN

Complete the chart below by rewriting part of your narrative using each narrative technique.

Narrative Technique	Rewrite
Dialogue	
Pacing	
Description	

Skill:
Transitions

sync•skills

••• CHECKLIST FOR TRANSITIONS

Before you revise your current draft to include transitions, think about:

- the order of events, including the rising action, climax, falling action, and resolution
- moments where the time or setting changes

Next, reread your current draft and note areas in your narrative where:

- the order of events is unclear or illogical
- changes in time or setting are confusing or unclear. Look for:

  > sudden jumps in time and setting

  > missing or illogical plot events

  > places where you could add more context to help the reader understand where and when plot events are happening

Revise your draft to use a variety of transition words, phrases, and clauses to convey sequence and signal shifts from one time frame or setting to another, using the following questions as a guide:

- Does my exposition provide necessary background information?
- Do the events of the rising action, climax, falling action, and resolution flow naturally and logically?
- Did I include a variety of transition words, phrases, and clauses that show sequence and signal setting and time changes?
- Transitions such as "that night" or "on the first sunny day" can indicate changes in time periods.
- Phrases or clauses such as "a week later, Bob boarded a train to Iowa" can indicate shifts in setting and time.

Please note that excerpts and passages in the StudySync® library and this workbook are intended as touchstones to generate interest in an author's work. The excerpts and passages do not substitute for the reading of entire texts, and StudySync® strongly recommends that students seek out and purchase the whole literary or informational work in order to experience it as the author intended. Links to online resellers are available in our digital library. In addition, complete works may be ordered through an authorized reseller by filling out and returning to StudySync® the order form enclosed in this workbook.

Reading & Writing
Companion

137

↻ YOUR TURN

Choose the best answer to each question.

1. Jalyn would like to add some transition words signaling that Anh lined up after the competition. Which transition phrase BEST shows the sequence of events in this passage?

> Anh lined up on the stage with the rest of the contestants.

- ○ A. At the end of the competition, Anh lined up on the stage with the rest of the contestants.
- ○ B. Before Anh lined up on the stage with the rest of the contestants, she went backstage.
- ○ C. In the community center, Anh lined up on the stage with the rest of the contestants.
- ○ D. Anh lined up on the stage, in front of the curtain, with the rest of the contestants.

2. Which passage from the Model below shows a strong transition in time period?

- ○ A. But when she got to the auditorium, Anh was overwhelmed with nerves. *What if I forget the words? Or worse, what if I open my mouth and forget how to sing?*
- ○ B. The following week, Anh sang with more energy than before, and grinned at her brother from the stage. *I can't wait to see the look on his face when I tell him about all those water slides . . .* she thought as she finished her song.
- ○ C. Jen's dad was so impressed that he suggested they enter a competition at their local community center. There would be a preliminary round in one month and a final round the following week.
- ○ D. When she went onstage, Anh was determined to give it her all. She felt the bright spotlights shining down on her, the crowd got silent, and she could hear the judges tapping their pencils and moving their papers.

↻ YOUR TURN

Complete the chart by revising a section of your narrative to include a shift in setting or time.

Transition In	Revision
Time	
Setting	
Time	
Setting	

Skill:
Conclusions

••• CHECKLIST FOR CONCLUSIONS

Before you write your conclusion, ask yourself the following questions:

- Which important details from my story should I summarize or remind readers of in my conclusion?
- What other thoughts and feelings could the characters share with readers in the conclusion?
- Should I express why the narrative matters through character reflections or dialogue?

Below are two strategies to help you provide a conclusion that follows from and reflects on the narrated experiences or events:

- Peer discussion

  > After you have written your introduction and body paragraphs, talk with a partner about possible endings for your narrative, writing notes about your discussion.

  > Review your notes and think about how you want to end your story.

  > Briefly summarize the events in the narrative through the narrator or one of the characters.

  > Describe how the narrator feels about the events he or she experienced.

  > Reveal to readers why the narrative matters through character reflections or dialogue.

  > Write your conclusion.

- Freewriting

  > Freewrite for ten minutes about what you might include in your conclusion. Don't worry about grammar, punctuation, or having fully formed ideas. The point of freewriting is to discover ideas.

  > Review your notes and think about how you want to end your story.

  > Briefly summarize the events in the narrative through the narrator or one of the characters.

  > Describe how the narrator feels about the events he or she experienced.

  > Reveal to readers why the narrative matters through character reflections or dialogue.

  > Write your conclusion.

↻ YOUR TURN

Read the excerpts below. Then, complete the chart by matching the correct strategy with each excerpt.

	Strategy Options
A	character or narrator's thoughts and feelings
B	important details to help summarize the story
C	reflections or dialogue to reveal why the narrative matters

Excerpt from *Stargirl*'s Conclusion	Strategy
We wanted to define her, to wrap her up as we did each other, but we could not seem to get past "weird" and "strange" and "goofy." Her ways knocked us off balance. A single word seemed to hover in the cloudless sky over the school: HUH? Everything she did seemed to echo Hillari Kimble: She's not real . . . She's not real . . .	
In that moonlit hour, I acquired a sense of the otherness of things. I liked the feeling the moonlight gave me, as if it wasn't the opposite of day, but its underside, its private side, when the fabulous purred on my snow-white sheet like some dark cat come in from the desert.	
It was during one of these nightmoon times that it came to me that Hillari Kimble was wrong. Stargirl *was* real.	

✏ WRITE

Use the questions in the checklist section to help you freewrite on the graphic organizer or on a piece of paper. Then revise the conclusion of your narrative.

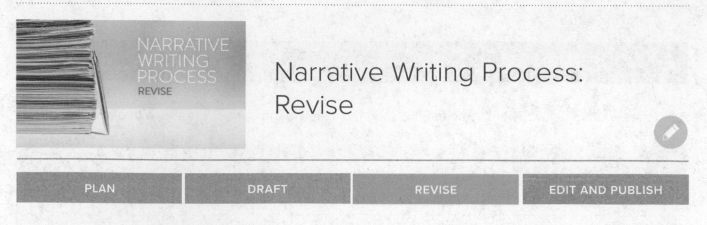

Narrative Writing Process: Revise

| PLAN | DRAFT | REVISE | EDIT AND PUBLISH |

You have written a draft of your narrative. You have also received input from your peers about how to improve it. Now you are going to revise your draft.

⤺ REVISION GUIDE

Examine your draft to find areas for revision. Keep in mind your purpose and audience as you revise for clarity, development, organization, and style. Use the guide below to help you review:

Review	Revise	Example
Clarity		
Identify places where some narrative techniques would improve your story. First, annotate any places where it is unclear who is speaking. Then, label each piece of dialogue so you know who is speaking.	Use the character's name to show who is speaking. Add description about the speaker.	"You control your voice well," ~~he said.~~ the second judge said. "Lots of nice touches in that song." *At least she was on key this time.*
Development		
Identify places where descriptive details are needed to describe important characters and the events of the plot. First, annotate places where vague or overused words are used. Then, annotate where you want to tell how something looks, sounds, feels, smells, or tastes.	Focus on a single event and add descriptive details, such as sensory details or precise action words.	But when she got to the auditorium, Anh was overwhelmed with nerves. She felt butterflies in her stomach, her mouth was dry, and she could only hear her heart. *What if I forget the words? Or worse, what if I open my mouth and forget how to sing?*

Review	Revise	Example
Organization		
Identify places where transitions would improve your story. First, reread and then retell your story. Then, annotate where there is a sudden jump in time and setting.	Rewrite the events in the correct sequence. Use transition words to signal changes in time or setting. Delete any events that are not essential to the story.	When she went onstage, Anh was determined to give it her all. She felt the bright spotlights shining down on her, the crowd got silent, and she could hear the judges tapping their pencils and moving their papers. She took a deep breath and felt the butterflies in her stomach disappear. As she started to sing, she was able to forget her nervousness and focus on the lyrics. ~~As she walked out on stage, she was determined to give it her all.~~ She stood taller and felt even more confident. She didn't miss a single beat! The crowd applauded loudly. Next, the judges weighed in.
Style: Word Choice		
Identify every form of the verb *to be* (*am, is, are, was, were, be, being, been*).	Select sentences to rewrite using action verbs.	Anh ~~was happy~~ smirked when she realized she'd be on all those rides at the park before Thao.
Style: Sentence Variety		
Think about a key event where you want your reader to feel a specific emotion. Long sentences can draw out a moment and make a reader think; short sentences can show urgent actions or danger.	Rewrite a key event making your sentences longer or shorter to achieve the emotion you want your reader to feel.	But Anh scored high, and so did Valeria and Jennifer. ~~They all scored high enough to make it to the second round so they could come back next week.~~ At the end of the competition they all made it to the second round.

✏️ WRITE

Use the guide above, as well as your peer reviews, to help you evaluate your narrative to determine areas that should be revised.

Grammar:
Basic Spelling Rules I

Spelling *ie* and *ei*

Spelling Conventions	Correct Spelling	Incorrect Spelling
Usually, when *i* and *e* appear together in one syllable, the *i* comes before the *e*.	siege wield fiend	seige weild feind
When *i* and *e* appear after a *c*, the *e* usually comes before the *i*.	conceive receiver	concieve reciever
However, there are exceptions to these patterns.	weird neither protein neighbor	wierd niether protien nieghbor

Suffixes and the Silent *e*

Spelling Conventions	Base Words	Correct Spelling	Incorrect Spelling
When adding a suffix that begins with a consonant to a word that ends with a silent *e*, keep the *e*.	amuse scene	amusement scenery	amusment scenry
When adding a suffix that begins with a vowel to a word that ends with a silent *e*, usually drop the *e*.	agile humane	agility humanity	agilety humanety

♻ YOUR TURN

1. How should the spelling error in this sentence be corrected?

> The Yukon region attracted the subspecies of humanity that would risk the harsh, unyeilding winters and seize any chance to strike it rich.

- ○ A. Change **subspecies** to **subspeceis**.
- ○ B. Change **unyeilding** to **unyielding**.
- ○ C. Change **seize** to **sieze**.
- ○ D. No change needs to be made to this sentence.

2. How should the spelling error in this sentence be corrected?

> César Chávez helped outlaw dangerous pesticides and end job discrimination, but his greatest achievement was bringing diverse people together to become activeists in a common cause.

- ○ A. Change **discrimination** to **discriminateion**.
- ○ B. Change **achievement** to **acheivement**.
- ○ C. Change **activeists** to **activists**.
- ○ D. No change needs to be made to this sentence.

3. How should the spelling error in this sentence be corrected?

> In the story "The Lottery," the most suspensful question is who will be chosen, but the most ominous element is the degree of acceptance by the villagers of this regular event.

- ○ A. Change **suspensful** to **suspenseful**.
- ○ B. Change **ominous** to **omenous**.
- ○ C. Change **acceptance** to **acceptence**.
- ○ D. No change needs to be made to this sentence.

Please note that excerpts and passages in the StudySync® library and this workbook are intended as touchstones to generate interest in an author's work. The excerpts and passages do not substitute for the reading of entire texts, and StudySync® strongly recommends that students seek out and purchase the whole literary or informational work in order to experience it as the author intended. Links to online resellers are available in our digital library. In addition, complete works may be ordered through an authorized reseller by filling out and returning to StudySync® the order form enclosed in this workbook.

Reading & Writing Companion **145**

Grammar:
Main and Subordinate Clauses

Main Clause

A clause is a group of words that includes both a subject and a verb (predicate). A clause may be a sentence by itself or part of a sentence.

A **main clause** is also called an independent clause because it expresses a complete thought and can stand alone as a sentence. Every sentence must have at least one main clause, and every main clause must have a subject and a verb. A main clause may be punctuated as a sentence.

Incorrect Main Clause	Correct Main Clause
won the meet	**Harrison won** the meet.
They cold hands	**They had** cold hands.

Subordinate Clause

Like a main clause, a **subordinate clause** must have a subject and a verb, but a subordinate clause does not express a complete thought and cannot stand alone as a sentence. A subordinate clause is also called a dependent clause, because it depends on a main clause to make sense.

Usually, a subordinating conjunction (such as *although, because, unless,* or *since*) introduces a subordinate clause, but the clause may also begin with a relative pronoun (*who, whose, whom, which, that,* or *what*) or adverb (*when, where,* or *why*).

Sentences can have a combination of clauses, but at least one must be a main clause. Two or more main clauses are commonly joined using a comma followed by a conjunction.

Clause	Sentence
Main Clause Subordinate Clause	**A good alternative is the roadside restaurant** where men gather for breakfast before going to work or going hunting. A good alternative is the roadside restaurant **where men gather for breakfast before going to work or going hunting**. *Travels with Charley*

↻ YOUR TURN

1 How should this sentence be revised?

> Rice dishes are easy to prepare they are popular in restaurants.

- ○ A. Insert a comma after the word *prepare*.
- ○ B. Remove the word *they*.
- ○ C. Insert a comma and the conjunction *and* after the word *prepare*.
- ○ D. The sentence does not need revision.

2. How should this sentence be revised?

> Alligators and crocodiles live in tropical regions because are cold-blooded.

- ○ A. Remove the word *in*.
- ○ B. Insert the word *they* after the conjunction *because*.
- ○ C. Replace the word *are* with the word *they*.
- ○ D. The sentence does not need revision.

3. How should this sentence be revised?

> Although many dinosaurs were calm plant-eaters, movies often portray dinosaurs as aggressive, horrifying carnivores.

- ○ A. Remove the word *Although*.
- ○ B. Insert the conjunction *but* after the first comma.
- ○ C. Insert the conjunction *and* after the second comma.
- ○ D. The sentence does not need revision.

4. How should this sentence be revised?

> Ancient people drew pictures on cave walls they wanted to record major events in their lives or because they needed to express their feelings.

- ○ A. Insert the word *when* after the word *walls*.
- ○ B. Remove the infinitive *to record*.
- ○ C. Change the conjunction *or* to the conjunction *and*.
- ○ D. The sentence does not need revision.

Grammar: Simple and Compound Sentences

A simple sentence has one complete subject and one complete predicate. The subject, the predicate, or both may be compound.

Simple Sentence
The ANTS were spending a fine winter's day drying grain collected in the summertime. *Aesop's Fables*

A compound sentence has two or more main clauses (simple sentences).
These main clauses are joined with a comma followed by a coordinating conjunction such as *or, and,* or *but*.
They can also be joined by a semicolon (;).

Compound Sentence	Coordinating Conjunction
Father was away on a trading expedition as usual, but our cook, Mandy, was there. *Ella Enchanted*	but

Compound Sentence	Coordinating Conjunction
You can tell he's real happy to have the bird-thing back, and his face isn't quite so fierce. *Freak the Mighty*	and

⟳ YOUR TURN

1   How can this sentence be changed into a simple sentence?

> Paramecium are very small a microscope is needed to examine them.

○ A. Insert a comma after **small**.

○ B. Insert a semicolon after **small**.

○ C. Remove the clause **a microscope is needed to examine them**.

○ D. No change needs to be made to this sentence.

2. How can this sentence be changed into a simple sentence?

> Liam had a solo in last year's concert, and he hopes to have one this year, too.

○ A. Remove the first comma, conjunction, and clause **he hopes to have one this year, too**.

○ B. Replace the first comma and conjunction with a semicolon.

○ C. Remove **in last year's concert**.

○ D. No change needs to be made to this sentence.

3. How can this sentence be changed into a compound sentence?

> Should I take the bus to school, or should I walk?

○ A. Change **or** to **but**.

○ B. Add **to school** after **walk**.

○ C. Change the comma to a semicolon.

○ D. No change needs to be made to this sentence.

4. How can this sentence be changed into a compound sentence?

> The storm blew down a tree on our street, there was no other damage.

○ A. Add the conjunction **but** after the comma.

○ B. Delete the comma and clause **there was no other damage**.

○ C. Remove the comma.

○ D. No change needs to be made to this sentence.

Narrative Writing Process: Edit and Publish

| PLAN | DRAFT | REVISE | EDIT AND PUBLISH |

You have revised your narrative based on your peer feedback and your own examination.

Now, it is time to edit your narrative. When you revised, you focused on the content of your narrative. You probably looked at your story's beginning, descriptive details, and narrative techniques. When you edit, you focus on the mechanics of your story, paying close attention to things like grammar and punctuation.

Use the checklist below to guide you as you edit:

☐ Have I followed spelling rules for words that use the suffix -*ed*?

☐ Have I checked for spelling mistakes in words that add a prefix?

☐ Have I checked that all sentences have a main clause?

☐ Do I have any sentence fragments or run-on sentences?

☐ Have I spelled everything correctly?

Notice some edits Jalyn has made:

- followed spelling rules for words that use the suffix -*ed*

- followed spelling rules for words that are commonly misspelled

- used a comma and a coordinating conjunction to connect two main clauses

- connected a subordinate clause to a main clause to create a complete sentence

> But Anh still loved music, and she kept playing every day. When she started middle ~~schoo.l she~~ school, she joined the choir. It became her favorite school activity. She and her friends had fun pretending to be reality-show singers on ~~weekends using~~ weekends, using a karaoke machine that belonged to Jennifer's family. Jen's dad was so ~~impresed~~ impressed that he suggested they enter a competition at their local community center. There would be a ~~prelimenary~~ preliminary round in one month and a final round the following week.

✏ WRITE

Use the questions on the previous page, as well as your peer reviews, to help you evaluate your narrative to determine areas that need editing. Then edit your narrative to correct those errors.

Once you have made all your corrections, you are ready to publish your work. You can distribute your writing to family and friends, hang it on a bulletin board, or post it on your blog. If you publish online, share the link with your family, friends, and classmates.

Please note that excerpts and passages in the StudySync® library and this workbook are intended as touchstones to generate interest in an author's work. The excerpts and passages do not substitute for the reading of entire texts, and StudySync® strongly recommends that students seek out and purchase the whole literary or informational work in order to experience it as the author intended. Links to online resellers are available in our digital library. In addition, complete works may be ordered through an authorized reseller by filling out and returning to StudySync® the order form enclosed in this workbook.

Reading & Writing
Companion

151

Ready for Marcos

FICTION

Introduction

Twelve-year-old Monica Alvarez has a happy life. She is a star on the track team and has many good friends. But everything changes when her parents bring Marcos, her new baby brother, home from the hospital. Her parents want her to have more responsibilities. Monica wonders what it will mean to be a big sister. Is she ready? Is she willing?

VOCABULARY

vivacious

energetic and happy; lively

justify

to support with good reasons

covertly

done in secret

subtle

barely noticeable

pursue

to try to do or achieve something

turmoil

a state of confusion, nervousness, or anxiety

☰ READ

— NOTES —

1 Three days ago, her parents brought him home from the hospital. From the time her mom and dad walked through the door with their sleeping bundle, everything was different. Her parents drifted through the day as if in a fog. They used to be energetic and **vivacious**, but now they seemed fatigued all the time.

2 On Marcos's fourth day home, Monica woke up and heard her parents talking quietly. She **covertly** walked to the door. "Monica is a big sister now," her dad said. "I think it's time for her to have more responsibilities around the house."

3 Her mom agreed. "We can talk to her at dinner," she added.

4 Monica turned and walked quietly back to her room. She closed the door behind her. *More responsibilities?* she thought to herself.

5 She spent much of the afternoon thinking about how the new baby would change her life. This year she was the fastest seventh grader on the track team. With more responsibilities, could she still **pursue** her dream of making the eighth-grade team? And what about time for her friends?

6 As dinner time grew closer, Monica began to fear the talk with her parents. She heard them cooking in the kitchen, so she ducked into his room where he was sleeping in his crib. Her new little brother—Marcos.

7 Monica looked at Marcos. She wondered how someone so small could **justify** such trouble. Then she looked closely at him. He was so small. She touched his soft cheek. *He's so cute*, Monica thought. Marcos opened his tiny eyes and looked up at her. As she looked at him, Monica felt a **subtle** change. Before she had felt in **turmoil**, but now she felt something new. She was a big sister. She knew how to tie her shoes and ride a bike. Marcos would need someone to show him how to do everything.

8 Later, Monica sat down to dinner. She felt her courage rise. "Mom, Dad, I have something to say," she began. "I'm a big sister now, and I should help more around the house." Her parents looked at each other. "I've done laundry lots of times," Monica explained, "and now I can do it for you and Marcos, too. Plus, I can help with dinner after track practice."

9 Her mom smiled. She said, "You're going to be the best big sister ever!"

First Read

Read the story. After you read, answer the Think Questions below.

1. Who is Marcos? How is he related to Monica?

   Marcos is _____.

   He is Monica's _____.

2. Why is Monica worried about making the track team?

   Monica worries that _____.

3. What does Monica promise to do to help her parents?

   Monica promises to _____.

4. Use context to confirm the meaning of the word *turmoil* as it is used in "Ready for Marcos." Write your definition of *turmoil* here.

   Turmoil means _____.

   A context clue is _____.

5. What is another way to say that someone *pursued* his or her dream?

   Someone _____.

Skill:
Analyzing Expressions

★ DEFINE

When you read, you may find English expressions that you do not know. An **expression** is a group of words that communicates an idea. Three types of expressions are idioms, sayings, and figurative language. They can be difficult to understand because the meanings of the words are different from their **literal**, or usual, meanings.

An **idiom** is an expression that is commonly known among a group of people. For example: "It's raining cats and dogs" means it is raining heavily. **Sayings** are short expressions that contain advice or wisdom. For instance: "Don't count your chickens before they hatch" means do not plan on something good happening before it happens. **Figurative** language is when you describe something by comparing it with something else, either directly (using the words *like* or *as*) or indirectly. For example, "I'm as hungry as a horse" means I'm very hungry. None of the expressions are about actual animals.

••• CHECKLIST FOR ANALYZING EXPRESSIONS

To determine the meaning of an expression, remember the following:

✓ If you find a confusing group of words, it may be an expression. The meaning of words in expressions may not be their literal meaning.

- Ask yourself: Is this confusing because the words are new? Or because the words do not make sense together?

✓ Determining the overall meaning may require that you use one or more of the following:

- context clues
- a dictionary or other resource
- teacher or peer support

✓ Highlight important information before and after the expression to look for clues.

⟳ YOUR TURN

Read the following excerpt from "Ready for Marcos." Then, complete the multiple-choice questions below.

---

from **"Ready for Marcos"**

Three days ago, her parents brought him home from the hospital. From the time her mom and dad walked through the door with their sleeping bundle, everything was different. Her parents drifted through the day as if in a fog. They used to be energetic and vivacious, but now they seemed fatigued all the time.

On Marcos's fourth day home, Monica woke up and heard her parents talking quietly. She covertly walked to the door. "Monica is a big sister now," her dad said. "I think it's time for her to have more responsibilities around the house."

---

1. What does "in a fog" in paragraph 1 mean?

   ○ A. The weather is bad.
   ○ B. The parents can't see.
   ○ C. The parents are upset.
   ○ D. The parents feel tired.

2. Which context clue helped you determine the meaning of the expression?

   ○ A. "They seemed fatigued all the time."
   ○ B. "Monica woke up and heard her parents talking quietly."
   ○ C. "Monica is a big sister now."
   ○ D. "She covertly walked to the door."

Skill:
Conveying Ideas

★ DEFINE

Conveying ideas means communicating a **message** to another person. When speaking, you might not know what word to use to convey your ideas. When you do not know the exact English word, you can try different strategies. For example, you can ask for help from classmates or your teacher. You may use gestures and physical movements to act out the word. You can also try using **synonyms** or **defining** and describing the meaning you are trying to express.

••• CHECKLIST FOR CONVEYING IDEAS

To convey ideas for words you do not know when speaking, use the following learning strategies:

- ✓ Request help.

- ✓ Use gestures or physical movements.

- ✓ Use a synonym for the word.

- ✓ Describe what the word means using other words.

- ✓ Give an example of the word you want to use.

⟳ YOUR TURN

Read the following excerpt from the story. Then imagine that someone is trying to convey the idea of Marcos *sleeping*. Find the correct example for each strategy to complete the chart below.

---

from "Ready for Marcos"

As dinner time grew closer, Monica began to fear the talk with her parents. She heard them cooking in the kitchen, so she ducked into his room where he was sleeping in his crib. Her new little brother—Marcos.

	Examples
A	The person explains that the word means "to rest."
B	The person closes their eyes and puts their head against the desk.
C	The person says, "This is when you close your eyes for a few minutes when you're tired, or when you lie in bed at night."
D	The person uses the similar word *napping*.

Strategies	Examples
Use gestures or physical movements.	
Use a synonym for the word.	
Describe what the word means using other words.	
Give examples of the word you want to use.	

Close Read

✏ WRITE

PERSONAL NARRATIVE: In "Ready for Marcos," Monica experiences a major change in her life. Tell about a big change in your own life. Tell why this was a big change for you. Describe how your life is now, using specific details. Pay attention to spelling patterns as you write.

Use the checklist below to guide you as you write.

☐ What is an event that has changed your life the most?

☐ What are some facts or details that you can give that show this was a big change?

☐ How is your life now?

Use the sentence frames to organize and write your personal narrative.

My life changed in a big way when _____.

It was important because _____.

I used to _____.

Now I _____.

Now my life is _____.

A World Away

FICTION

Introduction

As Rajeet Basak was about to begin seventh grade in Mumbai, India, his family moved to Chicago, Illinois, for his father's work. Rajeet had to learn to live in a new place. At the end of his first school year, he is interviewed by a reporter for the school newspaper about his experiences in his first year in Chicago. Rajeet explains that some things about the two places are different and some things are the same. What does Rajeet find strange? What does Rajeet think about life in Chicago?

 VOCABULARY

adjustment
a small, helpful change

announce
to tell people about something important

positive
good, happy, satisfied

bulky
heavy, hard to move

interview
a formal meeting in which a person answers questions

thermometer
instrument that measures heat and cold

≡ READ

1 A World Away

2 by Karen Dennison

3 This year Lakeside Middle School welcomed Rajeet Basak from Mumbai, India. His first year in Chicago was full of **adjustments**, but Rajeet is happy. His experience has been **positive**.

4 In an **interview**, Rajeet explained how he learned about his family's move. "I came home for dinner," Rajeet said. "During dinner, my father **announced** that we'd be moving to Chicago in a few weeks. I was in shock. I couldn't eat."

5 Rajeet did not know how different life would be. In Chicago he was lonely and sad at first. But then October came. Rajeet could think of nothing but the cold. He did not know how soon the long winter would begin.

6   Rajeet said, "We knew it was colder here than in Mumbai. So my mom and I went shopping for a winter coat. It felt heavy and **bulky**. It was hard to move in, but I was glad to have it!"

7   One day Rajeet looked at the **thermometer**. He could not believe the reading was so low. And he could not believe that he saw snow falling. "I didn't know what was happening," Rajeet remembered. "I'd read about snow, but I had never seen it. It was beautiful, but it was freezing cold when I touched it with bare hands. Now I wear gloves lined with wool."

8   The weather was a big shock to Rajeet. His first weeks were lonely. However, Rajeet has new friends. He met them through his interest in sports. "Some sports are the same. Others are not. My friends and I still play soccer. In India, soccer is called "football." Here, there's another sport called football. It is unlike anything I've ever seen! We watch it on TV."

9   Rajeet added that school in Chicago is somewhat different. "In Mumbai, we had bigger classes, but I like it here. I've tried to be respectful to my teachers as we were in Mumbai and as my friends are here."

10 Rajeet also likes American food. "It's less spicy, and there's more meat. But my mom still makes the same things we ate in Mumbai. It's not hard to find Indian spices, and I love a dish of chicken curry."

11 Rajeet has adapted to life here and learns more every day. Next year he hopes to join the soccer team and hopes for a milder winter.

First Read

Read the story. After you read, answer the Think Questions below.

☁ THINK QUESTIONS

1. Where did Rajeet live before his family moved?

   Rajeet lived in _____.

2. Why was life in Chicago difficult at first for Rajeet?

   Life in Chicago was difficult because _____.

3. What hopes does Rajeet have for next year?

   Rajeet hopes _____.

4. Use context to confirm the meaning of the word *bulky* as it is used in "A World Away." Write your definition of *bulky* here.

   Bulky means _____.

   A context clue is _____.

5. What is another way to say that an experience is *positive*?

   An experience is _____.

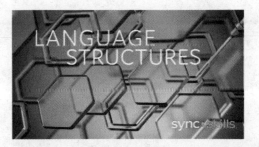

Skill:
Language Structures

★ DEFINE

In every language, there are rules that tell how to **structure** sentences. These rules define the correct order of words. In the English language, for example, a **basic** structure for sentences is subject, verb, and object. Some sentences have more **complicated** structures.

You will encounter both basic and complicated **language structures** in the classroom materials you read. Being familiar with language structures will help you better understand the text.

••• CHECKLIST FOR LANGUAGE STRUCTURES

To improve your comprehension of language structures, do the following:

✓ Monitor your understanding.

- Ask yourself: Why do I not understand this sentence? Is it because I do not understand some of the words? Or is it because I do not understand the way the words are ordered in the sentence?

✓ Break down the sentence into its parts.

- In English, most sentences share the same pattern: subject + verb + object.
  > The subject names who or what is doing the action.
  > The verb names the action or state of being.
  > The object answers questions such as Who?, What?, Where?, and When?

- Ask yourself: What is the action? Who or what is doing the action? What details do the other words provide?

✓ Confirm your understanding with a peer or teacher.

⟳ YOUR TURN

Read the following excerpt from the text. Then, complete the chart by writing the words and phrases into the "Subject," "Verb," and "Object" columns. The first row has been done as an example.

---

from "A World Away"

The weather was a big shock to Rajeet. His first weeks were lonely. However, Rajeet has new friends. He met them through his interest in sports. "Some sports are the same. Others are not. My friends and I still play soccer. In India, soccer is called "football." Here, there's another sport called football. It is unlike anything I've ever seen! We watch it on TV."

Sentence	Subject	Verb	Object
The weather was a big shock to Rajeet.	The weather	was	a big shock to Rajeet
However, Rajeet has new friends.			
Some sports are the same.			
My friends and I still play soccer.			
We watch it on TV.			

Skill: Retelling and Summarizing

★ DEFINE

You can retell and summarize a text after reading to show your understanding. **Retelling** is telling a story again in your own words. **Summarizing** is giving a short explanation of the most important ideas in a text.

Keep your retelling or summary **concise**. Only include important information and keywords from the text. By summarizing and retelling a text, you can improve your comprehension of the text's ideas.

••• CHECKLIST FOR RETELLING AND SUMMARIZING

In order to retell a story or summarize text, note the following:

✓ Identify the main events of the story.

- Ask yourself: What happens in this text? What are the main events that happen at the beginning, the middle, and the end of the text?

✓ Identify the main ideas in a text.

- Ask yourself: What are the most important ideas in the text?

✓ Determine the answers to the six *Wh-* questions.

- Ask yourself: After reading this text, can I answer Who?, What?, Where?, When?, Why?, and How? questions.

↻ YOUR TURN

Read the following excerpt from "A World Away." Then, write each event in the beginning, middle, or end of the chart to retell what happened in the story.

---

from **"A World Away"**

In an interview, Rajeet explained how he learned about his family's move. "I came home for dinner," Rajeet said. "During dinner, my father announced that we'd be moving to Chicago in a few weeks. I was in shock. I couldn't eat."

Event Options		
Rajeet is in shock and can't eat.	Rajeet came home for dinner	Rajeet's father says they are moving.

Beginning	
Middle	
End	

Close Read

✏ WRITE

ARGUMENTATIVE—LITERARY ANALYSIS: For Rajeet, life in Chicago is very different from his life in Mumbai. Did Rajeet adapt to his new life in Chicago? Support your response with events and evidence from the text. Make connections to your own experiences. Pay attention to subject-verb agreement as you write.

Use the checklist below to guide you as you write.

☐ What was Rajeet's life like before?

☐ What is Rajeet's life like now?

☐ What changes did Rajeet make in Chicago?

☐ What changes have you made to adapt to new things in your life?

Use the sentence frames to organize and write your literary analysis.

In Mumbai, there were _____.

In Chicago, the weather is _____.

At first, Rajeet is _____.

Then he makes new _____.

This reminds me of when I _____.

It was different because _____.

I adapted by _____.

PHOTO/IMAGE CREDITS:

studysync®

Text Fulfillment Through StudySync

If you are interested in specific titles, please fill out the form below and we will check availability through our partners.

ORDER DETAILS

Date:

TITLE	AUTHOR	Paperback/ Hardcover	Specific Edition *If Applicable*	Quantity

SHIPPING INFORMATION

Contact:

Title:

School/District:

Address Line 1:

Address Line 2:

Zip or Postal Code:

Phone:

Mobile:

Email:

BILLING INFORMATION   ☐ *SAME AS SHIPPING*

Contact:

Title:

School/District:

Address Line 1:

Address Line 2:

Zip or Postal Code:

Phone:

Mobile:

Email:

PAYMENT INFORMATION

☐ CREDIT CARD

Name on Card:

Card Number: Expiration Date: Security Code:

☐ PO

Purchase Order Number:

StudySync Text Fulfillment, BookheadEd Learning, LLC
610 Daniel Young Drive | Sonoma, CA 95476